Ecosystem Leadership
An approach for schools

Neil Barker

Published in 2025 by Amba Press, Melbourne, Australia
www.ambapress.com.au

First published in 2022 by ACER Press, an imprint of
Australian Council for Educational Research Ltd

In the spirit of reconciliation, Amba Press acknowledges the Traditional Custodians of Country throughout Australia and their connections to land, sea and community. We pay our respect to their elders past and present and extend that respect to all Aboriginal and Torres Strait Islander Peoples today.

© 2025 Neil Barker

This book is copyright. All rights reserved. Except under the conditions described in the Copyright Act 1968 of Australia and subsequent amendments, and any exceptions permitted under the current statutory licence scheme administered by Copyright Agency Limited (www.copyright.com.au), no part of this publication may be reproduced, stored in a retrieval system, transmitted, broadcast or communicated in any form or by any means, optical, digital, electronic, mechanical, photocopying, recording or otherwise, without the written permission of the publisher.

Edited by Michaela Skelly
Cover design, text design and typesetting by Karen Wilson
Cover image © Rawpixel.com; Monkey Business Images; fizkes @ shutterstock.com

ISBN: 9781923569201 (pbk)
ISBN: 9781923569218 (ebk)

A catalogue record for this book is available from the National Library of Australia.

About the author

Neil Barker is the former director of the Bastow Institute of Educational Leadership. He has more than 40 years' experience in the education sector, working in juvenile justice settings, specialist and primary schools, at the Melbourne Zoo, as a school principal and in education policy development.

Neil is currently the co-founder and director of LERNA Digital Learning and is involved in several international education networks. He is also a fellow of the Australian Council for Educational Leaders.

Acknowledgements

My first thought when asked to consider writing a book was, 'Who? Me?' And my response was, 'I've never written a book before, but I'll have a go.'

With sage advice from my mentor and friend Steve Munby and from ACER Press Publisher Elisa Webb, plus encouragement from my wonderful family, friends and colleagues (including you, Tony Mackay), I set forth in early 2020.

For 2 and a half years, I lost myself in a sea of reading, researching, and writing – bliss! My companion Clarrie (the dog) and I pushed our way through periods of doubt, writer's block and almost giving it away. I wouldn't have got here without the feedback from Steve Munby who helped me find my voice and has written a very kind foreword, and Lisa Black who told me I was definitely onto something.

I've often seen authors thanking their publishers and editors – I like that, and now have a deeper understanding of why – thank you so much Elisa, Shaneen and Michaela. I feel like I've had a lovely, warm publishing blanket wrapped around me for the last 2 years.

There are people in life who are critical to who we are. For me, it is 2 strong, passionate and intelligent women – my mother, Noelene, and my amazing wife, Bernadette. Without Bernadette's support and critical insights into my writing, I might have given up – thank you for that, but more, for being my friend.

Neil Barker
Living and working on Wurundjeri land
– always was and always will be Aboriginal Land.

Contents

	About the author	iii
	Acknowledgements	iv
	Foreword	vii

SECTION 1

INTRODUCTION	Leadership, leadership and leadership	3
CHAPTER 1	Ecosystem leadership	9
CHAPTER 2	An ecosystem approach to school leadership	25
CHAPTER 3	Building an ecosystem leadership approach	39

SECTION 2

CHAPTER 4	Leadership context	49
CHAPTER 5	Leadership vision	77
CHAPTER 6	Leadership processes	93
CHAPTER 7	Leadership focuses	107
CHAPTER 8	Leadership impact	119
CHAPTER 9	An integrated leadership ecosystem	135

	An endnote	143
	References	144

Foreword

Have you ever been on the receiving end of decisions in a school without understanding why or how they were made? Have you ever seen good, talented senior leaders that work well as individuals but seem to be pulling in different directions? Do you know of schools where a new leader came in full of ideas that were effective in their last school but who failed to gain a deep understanding of the school community and its challenges and context, with disastrous results? Or a school where the leadership used to be effective but gradually, over time, failed to adapt to the changing external context?

Ecosystem leadership addresses these problems, and others, head-on. Most books on school leadership are targeted at the individual leader and help us to reflect on how we can be more effective in our leadership. These books have their place, but *Ecosystem leadership* goes deeper, addressing whole-school culture and collective leadership.

When I was CEO of the National College for School Leadership in England in 2007, we concluded that our leadership development program for middle leaders in schools was limited in its impact and, to be honest, not a good use of public money. No matter how good the program was (and it was rated very highly by participants), its overall impact would, inevitably, be minimal. This was because the development program failed to consider sufficiently that the individual leader would be going back to a whole-school environment with its own systems, context and ways of working. The prevailing culture in the school will always override the impact of an individual leadership development program unless there is a whole-school approach towards leadership. At the National College for School Leadership, we had to shift our thinking away from focusing primarily on the individual and towards seeing leadership development as a whole-school issue. I think we would have realised this more quickly if Neil's book had been around at the time.

In this book, Neil moves the thinking about leadership forward and gives it an important new perspective. He considers schools as ecosystems, arguing that all aspects of a school and its community are interrelated and that to focus just on the individual leader is to fail to see the whole picture. Everyone in a school has a formal or informal leadership role and unless we look in a coherent way at leadership across the whole school community, any changes in individual leadership may or may not be helpful. It would be like focusing on a particular forest without considering the impact of climate change or considering changing the lifestyle and habitation of the wildebeest without thinking about the impact on lions.

Not only does *Ecosystem leadership* explain how the need for a collective approach to school leadership is strongly supported by the research evidence, but also it contains several practical activities that groups in a school can work on together to help to develop their collective leadership ecosystem.

I have known Neil for many years, mainly in his capacity as CEO of the Bastow Institute of Educational Leadership in Victoria. His compassionate and thoughtful leadership approach shines through this book, and we are treated to several reflective examples from his own considerable leadership experience.

If you are serious about impactful school leadership that goes beyond feelings and froth and looks deeply into tough and challenging whole-school issues, then this is the book for you.

Steve Munby

SECTION 1

INTRODUCTION
Leadership, leadership and leadership

Leadership is a curious thing. It can be as individual as our fingerprints, it can be different in different contexts, it can change as we learn and grow, it can involve people or projects, it can be official or unofficial, it can be earned or bestowed. Leadership can be joyous or sad, hard or easy, rewarding or disappointing, it can be individual or collective, and it can be a mix of all these and more.

There are things that leaders do that are successful and make significant difference, and there are things that leaders do that are not successful and make little difference. Leadership can be a waste of time, or it can make a difference. The evidence tells us that under particular conditions, leadership in schools has a significant impact on student outcomes.[1]

Leadership is personal, acknowledging our differing interests, needs, ideas, passions and experiences. Our leadership practices are influenced by a range of factors, including our organisational and community contexts, the role and mission of our organisation, our career stage, opportunities for development, our leadership role, the teams we are a part of or lead, the authorising environment we work in and the colleagues we work with. No matter what career stage we are at, we can all remember the lessons we have learnt from the things we have done, the mistakes we have made and the successes we have had. We are a sum of these experiences and how we lead is a complex interplay between these experiences, who we are and the nature of the place in which we are a leader.

---

1   Seashore LK, Leithwood K, Wahlstrom K and Anderson S (2010) *Learning from leadership learning: the links to improved student learning*, Wallace Foundation; Robinson VM, Lloyd, CA and Rowe KJ (2008) 'The impact of leadership on student outcomes: an analysis of the differential effects of leadership types', *Educational Administration Quarterly*, 44(5):635–674.

My first formal leadership experience was when I was appointed school captain at primary school. It was a surprise to me, I must say, and I could not understand why they had selected me. I wasn't gregarious or one of the 'in' crowd, I wasn't bossy or one of the sporty or popular people. In fact, I was a bit of a nerd. Clearly, the teachers could see something in me that I couldn't. Being a school captain was no great burden (well, I don't remember it being so). In fact, all I remember was giving a few short speeches when politicians turned up to school assemblies.

As my life and career progressed, there were opportunities to engage in various leadership opportunities of an informal and a formal nature, including as a classroom teacher, a senior teacher, an assistant principal, a principal, a leader of school network functions, and as an Education Policy Manager and Director of the Bastow Institute of Educational Leadership (Bastow Institute).

I had the pleasure of working with a broad variety of people in a great range of circumstances in the education sector. Some of the people I led with and for, and was led by, were great leaders, some were terrible, and some were just okay. Good, bad or indifferent, effective or ineffective, no 2 of these leaders led in the same way. They each brought themselves and their strengths and weaknesses, their biases, their passions and their lived experiences to their leadership and to the circumstances in which they were leading. In every workplace I have been in, there has been a wide diversity of leadership approaches, styles and practices. These and many other experiences influenced how I led and how I learnt and grew in my leadership practice, dispositions and knowledge.

If I look at my career and the development of my leadership skills, knowledge and capabilities, it feels as though I just fell into many of these experiences; sure, I did apply for many of the positions I was appointed to, but I do not recall being particularly strategic or intentional about my leadership and my leadership development. Much of my leadership learning was on the job and happened when I was appointed, but rarely did I discuss leadership with my fellow leaders or with my colleagues and stakeholders more broadly. I can remember few, if any, times in which I had explicit conversations with the people I was working with about our 'style' of and 'approach' to leadership, and how we might integrate our leadership approaches in our workplace.

In recent years I have been thinking more about the differences in leadership approach and style, and whether it is important that we harness this diversity of leadership style and practice in schools. Is it okay for each of the school's leaders to lead in different ways, to lead differently at different times, to lead differently in common areas in the school, or across the school, with the same people, or with different people? Is uniformity of leadership practice desirable or not? Should it be the same in particular circumstances or at certain times? Or is it okay for leadership to vary within and across a school?

The answers to all these questions are yes and no. There are advantages in allowing individual leaders to be true to themselves and to lead in a manner that is aligned with who they are, and there are advantages in ensuring that leadership across a school is consistent; that there is coherence in the way decisions are made, and leadership operates. The challenge is in designing a system that allows for both; an approach that integrates individual and collective school leadership.

Increasingly over the past 20 years, I have noticed that school leaders have been engaged in understanding more about themselves and their leadership through various professional learning activities, including through personality tests and work preference instruments (see Chapter 5 'Understand your leadership style' [p. 79]). In many cases, the results of these experiences have been shared by a team of leaders, so they can better understand each other and how they can work more effectively together. In my experience, these sorts of activities have not resulted in lasting differences in the way the team operated and more importantly did not lead to greater consistency or coherence in the way in which the leaders in the organisation practised their leadership. In fact, I cannot really remember any professional learning that I was involved in at a school or education facility that led to a more integrated, collective and 'whole of organisation' approach to leadership; an approach that would blend individual leadership styles into more systematic and coordinated leadership within, across and beyond a school.

It is my contention in this book that if we want to improve leadership in our schools then we need to better understand how we can lead more effectively together. We need to be more intentional about the school's leadership, particularly as it applies to a school's unique context. We cannot continue to be ad hoc in our approach to leadership within and across the school; we need to be more explicit about how we lead as a group of leaders, about our leadership intentions, about our leadership focuses and about how we will improve leadership in our schools. We cannot leave leadership to chance.

Schools spend a great deal of time planning how we will implement our curriculum, how we will allocate our funds, how we structure our teaching workforce, what our strategic plan will focus on and how we will improve learning and teaching. But how much time do we spend agreeing on our approach to leadership? The evidence is clear about the impact of leadership on improving student learning outcomes,[2] and yet many schools spend little time on developing their school-wide approach to leadership: little time on creating a leadership system relevant to their unique circumstances; little time developing a collective way to lead improved student learning.

Imagine the benefits of explicit, agreed and consistent leadership efforts in a school; effort that is comprehensive, transparent and contextualised. Consider the potential payback for staff, students, parents, the broader school community and education system, and for the leaders themselves of a locally developed and agreed school leadership approach in which individual and collective leadership effort is integrated and coherent.

This book outlines an approach for developing an integrated system of leadership in our schools. It provides a framework to assist schools to develop a leadership system that is deliberate, consistent and comprehensive; leadership design and practice that ensures school leaders can work together in more coherent and coordinated ways to improve student outcomes. While this book focuses on schools, the concepts described could be applied to any organisation interested in creating a more systematic and collaborative approach to leadership.

Chapter 1 discusses how natural ecosystems and leadership approaches can work together to form an ecosystem leadership approach. It introduces the 3 key ecosystem attributes, and the 5 ecosystem leadership elements.

---

2   Seashore et al. (2010)

Chapter 2 looks in depth at the elements of the ecosystem leadership framework and the attributes of natural ecosystems.

Chapter 3 explores an integrated system of leadership: discussing school leadership considerations, how to implement an ecosystem approach to school leadership, and steps for building a leadership ecosystem.

Chapters 4 to 8 explore each of the ecosystem leadership elements in greater depth, providing detail about the fundamental elements of each domain, how it might look in practice, and how they might be developed and implemented.

Chapter 9 explores how a school can integrate the various elements of the approach to develop a fit-for-purpose, context-aligned leadership ecosystem that is directly focused on improving school and student outcomes.

CHAPTER 1
Ecosystem leadership

Natural ecosystems
One of the things that has intrigued me throughout my life is the way in which the natural environment operates. I was inspired by my biology teacher's passion for our planet's systems and processes. I have often used the foundational knowledge I gained at school to consider how I might create similar organisational systems in the places I have worked.

For millions of years, our planet has successfully created a global network of interactive ecosystems that ensure the effective and efficient management of the natural environment – systems that operate across the world in differing climatic zones, at various altitudes and in particular topographical areas; systems that operate across large geographical regions or small microcosms of a system, and systems that operate everywhere in between these 2 extremes. Typically, ecosystems have processes and interrelationships that enhance the operation of that community; they operate in a way that benefits all members of that system. Desert, rainforest and wetland ecosystems, for example, are very different in terms of the characteristics of each of those systems, but they have a variety of common processes that build, sustain, grow and enhance each.

While there is a diversity of views about what constitutes an ecosystem, the commonly accepted definition of an ecosystem is a collection of living and non-living elements that exist together in a particular place with a variety of interrelationships operating between the system's elements.[1] Ecosystems are dynamic and self-sustaining and usually include:

---

1   Britannica (n.d.) Ecosystem, accessed 27 July 2020. https://www.britannica.com/science/ecosystem

- a diversity of components
- a range of interactions and interdependencies
- processes and cycles that support the health and development of the system
- interaction with the surrounding biosphere.

The key characteristics of an ecosystem can be divided into 3 main attributes (see Figure 1.1): the constituent parts of the system (its membership); the interactions, cycles and processes that operate within and beyond the system (its operation) and the context in which the system operates; the system's relationship with other systems (its connectivity).

Leadership approaches

So, why not take the same systemic approach to leadership in a school? Why not create a 'leadership ecosystem' with interconnected components that work together for the health and development of the school and its constituent parts? Perhaps using the concept of a natural ecosystem can help us to create leadership across a school that is dynamic and self-sustaining; a leadership system that successfully integrates a diversity of components, and a range of interactions and interdependencies; a system that customises its leadership processes and cycles to suit local conditions, and that can manage interactions with the external school environment for mutual benefit.

I have worked in schools where the leadership approach did come close to developing practices that were 'systematic' and 'integrated', and others where the approach was ad hoc. In one school, with a successful 'leadership system', the staff had a strong commitment to the vision and mission of the organisation, the leadership structure was 'flat' (not overly hierarchical) and there was good communication and interaction between staff who all led various aspects of the school's improvement (whether they were in a formal or informal leadership role). A great deal was achieved, and the school had a good reputation. While much of this leadership approach was not necessarily intentional, it did show what is possible when the staff in an organisation are clear about what that organisation is seeking to achieve, has a strong commitment to

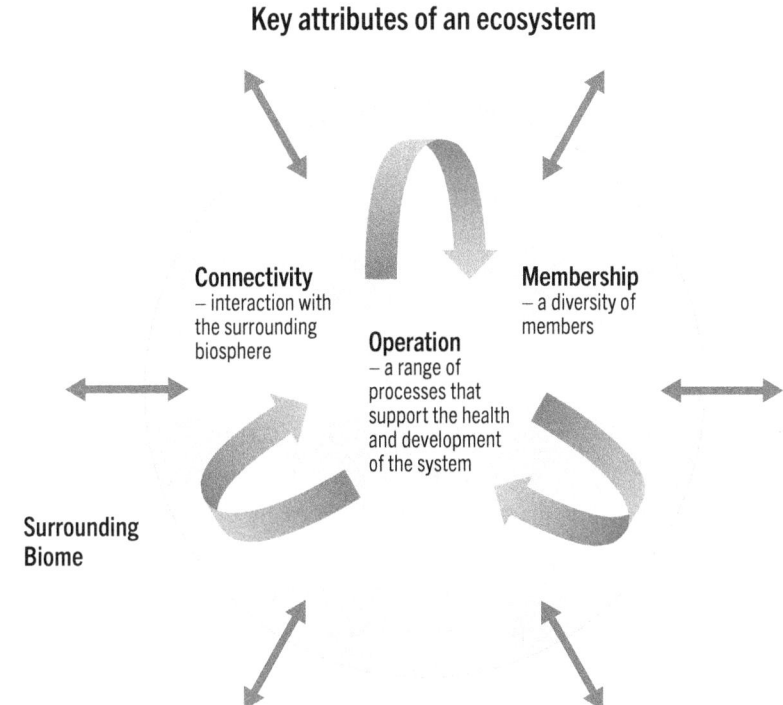

Figure 1.1 Key attributes of an ecosystem – membership, operation, connectivity

the mission of the organisation, and where the organisation's 'formal' leaders practice inclusive and collaborative leadership.

Using ecosystem principles to structure our leadership approach in schools provides us with a unique opportunity to create a more holistic leadership system, to reflect on how we approach leadership and to consider how we can more effectively focus our leadership effort on improving school and student outcomes (see Chapters 8 and 9).

The approach outlined in this book is much more than just undertaking ad hoc individual leadership learning exercises or engaging in team-building processes. It is about being more systematic about how we agree to lead, how we lead and how we know whether leadership at our school is making a difference. It is a planning, implementation and improvement approach for leadership within, across and beyond a school.

'Ecosystem leadership' challenges us to consider how well we are integrating aspects of leadership in our school, how connected the parts of the system are, how well our leadership processes and systems work, and how well our leadership practice is aligned to the internal and external contexts of the school. It provides us with an opportunity to bring our leadership effort into alignment – individual and collective, formal and informal, positional and non-positional – to create an integrated leadership ecosystem.

Ecosystems + leadership

So how can the elements of an ecosystem provide guidance around how leadership might work in a school? This book uses the 3 key ecosystem attributes identified in Figure 1.1 on p. 11 to frame a more systematic approach to leadership in a school; integrating the membership parts of a leadership system, creating processes that ensure effective and efficient system operation, and ensuring that leadership considers a school's internal and external contexts and interactions between the 2.

Across the 3 'ecosystem attributes', I have identified 5 'leadership elements' that consider a school's *membership*, *operation* and *connectivity*. These 5 leadership elements each fall within the 3 ecosystem attributes (see Figure 1.2):

1. *Leadership context* – the internal and external nature and circumstances of the ecosystem.
   Understanding internal and external school circumstances to create the foundations of a leadership approach that is aligned with the needs, interests and aspirations of a school community. Every school is different, and its leadership approach should reflect local conditions.
2. *Leadership vision* – the overarching purpose and foundational principles of the ecosystem design and operation.
   Creating a shared *vision* of, and *principles* for, leadership at the school; creating clarity for both leaders and followers about what leadership stands for and how it should operate at the school.

3. *Leadership processes* – the interconnections and systems within and beyond the ecosystem.
   Establishing clear, effective and consistent *processes* that ensure leadership practice at the school is efficient, comprehensive and coherent.
4. *Leadership focuses* – the emphases and priorities of the system's operation.
   Agreeing on a set of *focuses* to ensure leadership effort is directed at the things that matter for the school and broader community and that are important for improving the school's leadership approach.
5. *Leadership impact* – improving the performance and impact of the system.
   Measuring and improving leadership performance and *impact* at a school, in the context of improving school and student outcomes.

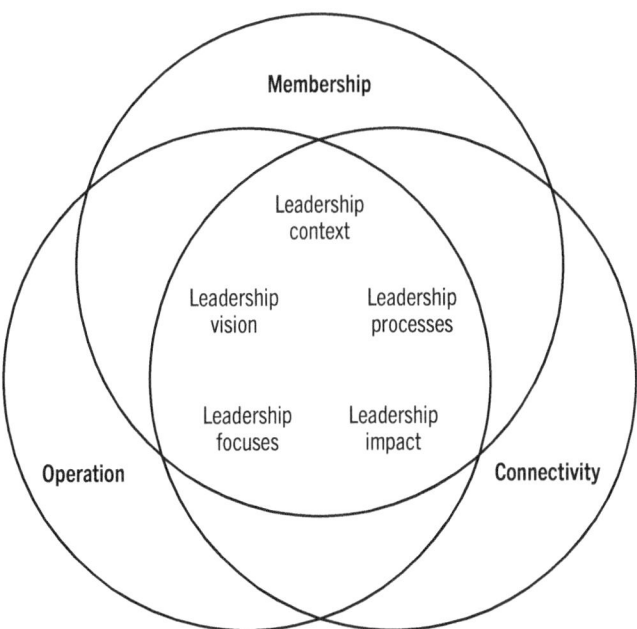

Figure 1.2 The relationship between the ecosystem attributes and the ecosystem leadership elements

An ecosystem approach to school leadership

As a principal I spent a great deal of time considering how to structure the school so that various aspects were led and managed effectively; grade levels, curriculum areas, school resources, programs, new initiatives, improvement focuses, student services, administrative and financial functions, school council and so forth. It was complex and I can remember spending a great deal of my time prior to the beginning of each year considering the previous year's leadership structure and operation and considering changes that would enhance how the school was led for the coming year. On reflection, I think I could have done a lot better; I think I could have been more systematic, strategic and consultative about the way the school's leadership approach was developed, agreed and implemented. This reflection, together with a range of other experiences across 30 years of leadership, has guided me in the development of the *ecosystem leadership approach* outlined in this book.

Critical to this leadership approach is that we consider both the design and operation of the leadership system at our schools. We should set out to intentionally create an approach that is based on data and best evidence, effective consultative practice and with reference to local and broader school contexts. We need systems and processes to measure the operation of our leadership practice and to understand the impact it has on refining and increasing the capacity for leadership to improve school and student outcomes. Subsequent chapters in this book speak more about the importance of having a clear and agreed leadership design and implementing systems for continuous improvement of the approach.

It is important to note that this approach does not preclude leaders from developing or using certain styles of leadership, nor does it mandate a particular style of leadership. There is a broad range of leadership styles:[2] autocratic, transactional, bureaucratic, transformational, servant, instructional, collective and situational. While understanding more about these can help us build a school leadership approach, it is critical that whatever style or approach to leadership is used by individuals, that their practice is consistent with the agreed approach at the school, and that both individual and collective school leadership practice are productive elements in the school's leadership 'ecosystem'. As Rose Amanchukuw and colleagues suggest, 'Leadership is not a "one size fits all" phenomenon. Leadership styles should be selected and adapted to fit organizations, situations, groups, and individuals'.[3]

While not the focus of this book, the development of individual leaders' leadership knowledge, skills and dispositions is important work for individuals, schools and education systems. The Principal Performance Improvement Tool[4] developed by the Australian Council for Educational Research (ACER) is an example of an important resource that can be used to improve the leadership capacity of a school leader. There is a broad range of short courses, seminars and longer term capability building courses that are available to school leaders at all levels of experience. The capacity of school leaders to improve their individual performance and to adjust their practice to suit various contexts and circumstances is a critical foundation for an effective collective school leadership approach.

A systematic and comprehensive approach to leadership must inherently involve a strong degree of leaders working together within, across and beyond the school. We never stand alone as a leader; we

---

2   Al Khajeh EH (2018) 'Impact of leadership styles on organizational performance', *Journal of Human Resources Management Research*, vol. 2018, article ID 687849, doi:10.5171/2018.687849; Amanchukwu RN, Nwachukwu OP and Stanley GJ (2015) 'A review of leadership theories, principles and styles and their relevance to educational management', *Management*, 5(1):6–14, accessed 18 June 2020. http://article.sapub.org/10.5923.j.mm.20150501.02.html - Sec4.5; Becker B (2022) 'https://blog.hubspot.com/marketing/leadership-styles', HubSpot blog, accessed 12 July 2022; Sendjaya S (2017) Why Australian businesses need to become servant leaders, Impact, Monash Business School, accessed 23 June 2020. https://impact.monash.edu/leadership/why-australian-business-leaders-need-to-become-servant-leaders/; Yasir M, Imran R, Irshad MK, Mohamed NA and Khan MM (2016) 'Leadership styles in relation to employees' trust and organizational change capacity: evidence from non-profit organizations', *SAGE Open*, doi:10.1177/2158244016675396
3   Amanchukwu et al. (2015:9)
4   ACER (Australian Council for Educational Research) (2018a) *Using the principal performance improvement Tool*, accessed 18 January 2022. https://research.acer.edu.au/tll_misc/31/

are connected in so many ways to the people around us, to the history of the organisation, to policies and priorities of the system in which we work, to the aspirations and hopes of the school community, to the capabilities and dispositions of our staff and fellow leaders.

Collective leadership

'Collective', 'shared' and 'distributed' leadership approaches are generally distinguished from other approaches by the fact that they are not 'top down' approaches; they describe the leader/follower relationship and leader/leader relationship in less formal and hierarchical ways; they include greater 'sharing' of the work and leadership, based on people's strengths; and they tend to be dynamic and agile in their application.[5]

There is increasing research and evidence about the effectiveness of *collective* leadership approaches.[6] Recent studies have shown that collective (or shared) leadership can predict team effectiveness[7] and lead to higher rates of leader engagement, commitment, leader-to-leader feedback, capacity to meet business challenges, and improved cultures

---

5   D'Innocenzo L, Mathieu JE and Kukenberger MR (2014) 'A meta-analysis of different forms of shared leadership – team performance relations', *Journal of Management*, 1–28, doi:10.1177/0149206314525205; Friedrich TL, Vessey WB, Schuelke MJ, Ruark GA and Mumford MD (2011) *Technical report 1288. A framework for understanding collective leadership: the selective utilization of leader and team expertise within networks*, US Army Research Institute for the Behavioural and Social Sciences, accessed 29 July 2022. https://arit.sirsi.net/uhtbin/cgisirsi/?ps=4rp3rkEb1a/0/X/60/495/X > technical report 1288; West M, Lyubovnikova J, Eckert R and Denis J-L (2014) 'Collective leadership for cultures of high quality health care', *Journal of Organizational Effectiveness: People and Performance*, 1(3):240–260

6   Hmieleski KM, Cole MS and Baron RA (2012) 'Shared authentic leadership and new venture performance', *Journal of Management*, 38:1476–1499, doi:10.1177/0149206311415419; Bolívar B, López Yáñez JF and Murillo J (2013) *School leadership. A review of current research perspectives*, accessed 10 February 2021. https://repositorio.uam.es > liderazgo en las instituciones educativas: una revisión de líneas de investigación; Pont B (2020) 'A literature review of leadership policy reforms', *European Journal of Education*, 55(2):154–168, https://doi.org/10.1111/ejed.12398; Angelle PS and DeHart CA (2016) 'Comparison and evaluation of four models of teacher leadership', *Research in Educational Administration & Leadership*, 1(1):85–119

7   West M, Armit K, Loewenthal L, Ecker R, West T and Lee A (2015) *Leadership and leadership development in healthcare: the evidence base*, Faculty of Medical Leadership and Management, London, UK, accessed 29 July 2022. www.kingsfund.org.uk > leadership development health care

and practice of professional learning, together with a lessened risk of leaders leaving an organisation.[8]

In terms of the specific impact of collective leadership in schools, Karen Seashore and colleagues found that 'Collective leadership has a stronger influence on student achievement than individual leadership'.[9] Of note in their findings around collective and shared leadership, is the importance of 'leader influence'. This influence can improve working relationships and professional community within a school and have an associated impact on student achievement or the conditions for improved student achievement. Critically, they also found that 'Principals and district leaders have the most influence on decisions in all schools; however, they do not lose influence as others gain influence'.[10]

Of course, working collectively is not always effective.[11] I am sure we have all experienced situations where working together is not particularly productive, and in fact at times it feels like it would just be easier and more effective to just do the work yourself. The challenge, of course, is to ensure the right conditions are in place so that the collective effort *is* productive.

The effectiveness of various leadership approaches will in part be influenced by the context in which that leadership operates, and the fidelity of development and implementation of the approach. What works in one school may not necessarily work in another or may require modification to be successful. Cassandra O'Neill and Monica Binkerhoff argue that 'Collective leadership requires specific conditions for the success of the whole: trust, shared power, transparent and effective communication, accountability, and shared learning'.[12] It may be that for a collective leadership approach to be successful, these (and

---

8   Canwell A, Rolland L and Cotton T (2018) 'Collective leadership: leading for value across organizational boundaries', *Global Leadership Forecast 2018*, DDI, The Conference Board and EY, accessed 4 August 2022. https://www.conference-board.org/publications/publicationdetail.cfm?publicationid=7717
9   Seashore et al. (2010:19)
10 Seashore et al. (2010:37)
11 D'Innocenzo et al. (2014)
12 O'Neill C and Brinkerhoff M (2018) 'Five elements of collective leadership', *Not-for-Profit Quarterly*, Boston, MA, accessed 24 June 2020. https://nonprofitquarterly.org/five-elements-collective-leadership/

other) conditions or elements are necessary in equal part, or in varying degrees, depending on the school and its nature and context.

But is collective leadership in and of itself sufficient, particularly if we examine and analyse the research and evidence and glean for ourselves what would work at our school? For that matter, why not just work our way through the literature on leadership and 'cherry pick' the bits that seem effective and relevant to our circumstances to organise our individual and agreed school approach to leadership?

While that may improve our individual and collective leadership capability and impact, it is argued here that we need to be more intentional than that in order to fully maximise the impact of leading collectively. We need to be more explicit and strategic about how we design, develop and implement our school's leadership approach to ensure that leadership effort drives improved school and student outcomes.

Developing a more holistic approach to leadership can help to improve the coherence, consistency and effectiveness of our leadership effort, replacing unconnected leadership practice with an interconnected system of leadership effort.[13] Collective leadership is an important part of a leadership ecosystem, and where, when and how it is used should be carefully considered as we develop a school's leadership design and practice.

Why use an ecosystem approach?

There are many potential benefits to using an 'ecosystem approach' for school leadership. It can assist us to improve leadership practice, be of benefit to the school community and can drive improved school and student outcomes. Some of the potential benefits are described here.

Leadership design and practice

Basing our leadership approach on the concept of an *integrated system* can help us to ensure that our approach is comprehensive in its design and implementation. A well-designed leadership ecosystem will ensure

---

[13] Stollar S, Poth R, Curtis M and Cohen R (2006) 'Collaborative strategic planning as illustration of the principles of systems change', *School Psychology Review*, 35(2):181–197

that all aspects of leadership in the school are a part of the system, that they are connected and that they operate productively together. A comprehensive system will circumvent disconnected leadership activity that is likely to create inefficiencies, confusion and inconsistencies in leadership application. The design will also provide guidance for leadership practice beyond the school, ensuring that the school's *context* and agreed *vision* and *principles* guide the leadership practice being undertaken on behalf of the school.

Consistency and coherence of leadership practice

Creating an agreed leadership design that applies to all leadership activity in a school ensures greater consistency in leadership practice and decision-making. Given that all school members will from time to time be involved in some form of formal or informal leadership activity, an agreed leadership design provides everyone with guidance about how they should operate when leading; be they a teacher, school support staff member, student or parent. It allows a school to document the leadership approach so that leaders are clear about how they are expected to lead and opens the school's leadership design and practice to scrutiny. It allows for the establishment of effective leadership feedback processes and for leadership to be held accountable for the way individual and collective school leadership practice and processes operate; it can facilitate a better understanding of *leadership impact* and can help to drive improved leadership design and practice.

Diversity of practice within a common framework

The approach outlined in this book does not prescribe or mandate a particular 'style' of leadership, but instead allows individuality in leadership practice within an agreed school leadership framework. Being explicit about the school's leadership approach allows school leaders to reflect on their leadership style and adjust their practice to fit with the school's approach. Occasionally, this may mean working with the school community to consider adjusting the approach or encouraging someone to seek a school that better reflects their leadership preferences.

Organisational design

Developing an agreed approach should include an examination of the school's current leadership characteristics and consideration of how leadership could be better constructed to ensure improved school and student outcomes. This will assist with considering which areas, initiatives or aspects of the school require formal leadership, how that leadership should be constructed, how it should operate and how it should connect with other parts of the school's leadership ecosystem. It will also contribute to creating leadership role clarity, understanding leadership spheres of influence and span of control, resourcing requirements and mapping decision-making processes.

Succession planning

Establishing an agreed school-wide leadership approach assists with leadership recruitment, selection processes and moderating the impacts of leadership staff turnover. It can provide clarity about the leadership approach for educators considering applying for leadership vacancies at the school and assist with framing and guiding recruitment processes. A clearly documented and well-implemented leadership design can provide certainty about the ongoing consistency and coherence of leadership practice when there are leadership changes at the school. It can provide a base from which to modify the leadership design when appointing new leaders and adapting to changes to *leadership context, focuses* and personnel.

Improved leadership practice

A systematic approach to leadership implies that the design and practice is not linear; that the approach includes a web of processes, cycles and practices that connect the various elements of the system and lead to a more integrated approach to leadership and leadership improvement. A connected system allows for a range of processes and systems to grow and develop leaders and leadership practice in a school. This could include opportunities for leaders to engage in cycles of leadership trial and error, the development of feedback processes and systems for measuring *leadership impact*; for leaders to be held to account for their performance against the design, to drive leadership learning to improve individual and collective school leadership practice; and to improve the leadership design itself.

Leadership efficiencies

Developing a school leadership approach provides an opportunity to review, modify or develop existing and new *leadership processes* and practices so that they operate more effectively and efficiently within, across and beyond the school. Ensuring, for example, that leadership effort is shared and allocated based on capability and need and that there are strong leadership connections between areas of the school can help avoid the doubling up of decision-making processes or outcomes or establish precedents and processes that can be used in other areas. Having more transparent processes can help reduce the guessing and speculation that occurs when people are unsure about the how or why of a leadership process. Having a clearly documented leadership approach can assist with the development of new leadership processes or practices to meet new or changing needs at the school.

Improved team efficacy

Teams can create efficiencies, construct manageable groups of people, provide opportunities for shared voice and enhanced communication, aid decision-making, provide focus and operational boundaries, enhance collaboration, assist in sharing ideas and workload, and provide a basis for evaluation and accountabilities processes. There is considerable research about the effectiveness of teams, the conditions that teams require to function effectively, and how to create, support and develop teams.[14] Wageman and colleagues, for example, outline 6 conditions that they have identified in their research of more than 120 senior leadership teams that account for close to 50 percent of the variation

---

14 National Research Council (2015) *Enhancing the effectiveness of team science*, The National Academies Press, Washington, DC; Kozlowski WJ and Ilgen DR (2006) 'Enhancing the effectiveness of work groups and teams', *Psychological Science in the Public Interest*, 7(3):77–124, doi:10.1111/j.1529-1006.2006.00030.x; Hattie J (2015) 'High impact leadership', *Educational Leadership*, 72(5):36–40, http://www.ascd.org/publications/educational_leadership/feb15/vol72/num05/High-Impact_Leadership.aspx

in the performance of those teams.[15] Careful, considered and nuanced application of team research and evidence can play an important part in improving *leadership impact* and *performance* in enhancing school and student outcomes.

Improved outcomes

Proving a direct causal relationship between a leadership action and improved student learning outcomes is a difficult process, given the number of variables, such as family circumstances, teacher practice and student class characteristics that exist between that action and a student outcome. However, as noted at the beginning of this chapter there is significant evidence about the impact of effective leadership on improving student achievement. Intentionally developing a clear, comprehensive and *integrated system of leadership* and effectively implementing that system creates a foundation from which to drive improved school and student outcomes. Surely our students deserve our every effort to establish leadership practices and processes that suit the needs, interests and aspirations of every school.

There are many instances in our lives when working together is more effective, efficient and rewarding for ourselves, for the people we work with and for achieving the outcomes we are seeking. It makes sense that we can achieve more by sharing the load, bringing different skill sets together, building on each other's effort and approaches, and by supporting and encouraging each other. One of the most rewarding leadership positions I have held is as coach and assistant coach of several AFL Women's teams. The collective approach in all these teams not only involved me and the other coaches, but the team managers, the club president and officials, the team captain and leadership team, and the players and their families. The experience for everyone involved was rich, inclusive, affirming and resulted in successful outcomes for the team, including a few grand final appearances and premierships. The strength here was the capacity of the club's leaders to share leadership and invite others in, as Mary Parker Follett in her work in the early 20th

---

15 Wageman R, Nunes D, Burruss J and Hackman R (2008) *Senior leadership teams: what it takes to make them great*, Harvard Business School Press, Boston, MA

century on 'management theory' argued, collective school leadership is 'power with others rather than power over others'.[16]

How do we create a leadership approach based on 'power *with* others', an approach that includes everyone who leads in a school irrespective of whether they are in a formal leadership position: teachers, students, education support workers, parents, formal and informal groups and teams, and anyone else associated with the school? How can we work together in more explicit and coordinated ways? What might this look like, how could it be developed, and how would we know if it was making a difference? What value might there be in developing a more collective approach to our leadership effort that operates as a leadership ecosystem?

Chapter 2 examines how ecosystems operate and explores how we might use some of the ideas inherent in *ecosystem operation* to create a collective school leadership system.

---

16 O'Neill and Brinkerhoff (2018)

CHAPTER 2
An ecosystem approach to school leadership

In Chapter 1 we discussed the place of ecosystems and how they provide us with examples of systems and processes that manage the natural environment in which we live. For millennia, these systems have operated complex processes and relationships that have maintained and grown various physical and living environments across the earth. These systems range from small, localised processes and arrangements to large planetary cycles and events: food chains and food webs, water cycles, decay cycles, weather and climate systems, erosion processes, energy systems and ecosystems.

We also briefly examined 3 attributes of a natural ecosystem: membership, operation and connectivity; and 5 associated ecosystem leadership elements that we can use to assist us to develop an integrated and intentional system of school leadership: context, vision, focuses, processes and impact (see Figure 2.1 on p. 26). These 5 elements can guide all leadership activity at a school: individual and collective, positional and non-positional, formal and informal, whole school and school unit leadership. They can assist with leadership as it applies to staff, students, parents and school community members, and with respect to leadership interactions outside the school.

To better understand how we can use the 'ecosystem leadership elements' to create an integrated framework of leadership practice at a school, let's have a closer look at each of the elements; what each includes, what it focuses on, why we would use it in our leadership design, and how we might use it.

Elements of the ecosystem leadership framework

Each of the leadership elements described here form an important part of a leadership system. How the interdependencies between each of

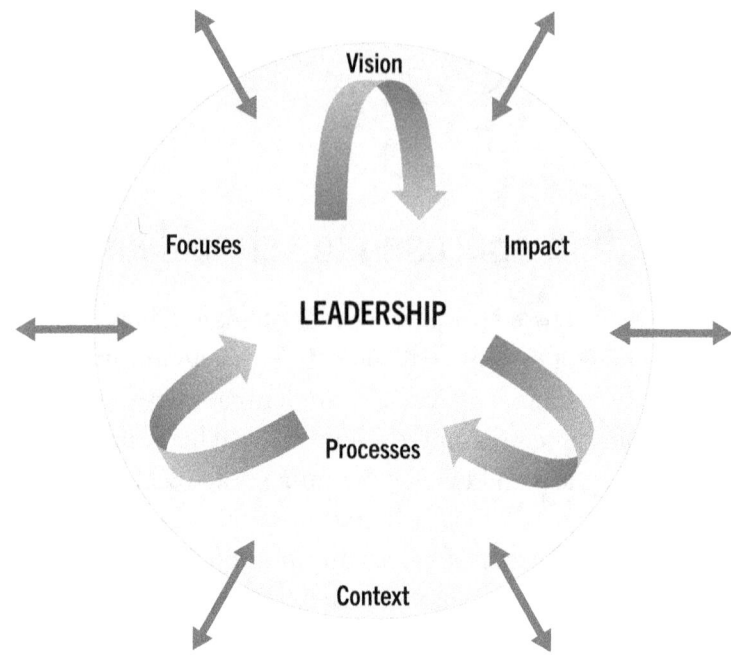

Figure 2.1 The 5 ecosystem leadership elements

these elements works is explored in Chapter 3. For now, let us look a little closer at what constitutes each of the elements.

1. Leadership context

- A school's leadership ecosystem should identify and analyse the internal and external contexts in which it operates to ensure that the school's leadership design and practice is aligned with the circumstances of that school and its broader community, ensuring that it is 'fit for purpose'; that it does what it was designed to do.
- Leadership context for schools is likely to include demographic, sociocultural, historical and performance information, together with the identified needs, interests and aspirations of that community, and the broader educational, economic, environmental and social systems in which the school operates.
- Leadership context should consider how the school's leadership approach is impacted by local and broader contexts and how the leadership approach impacts on those contexts.

- Leadership context development will benefit from the development of an explicit stakeholder management plan. It is important to identify who has an interest in and an impact on a school and its leadership, and anyone or any organisation that will be impacted by what the school does and how leadership operates. Identifying and planning for how leadership will interact with the key stakeholders that are a part of a school's context will ensure that leadership relationships within, across and beyond the school are successfully harnessed and managed.

2. Leadership vision
- A leadership vision and associated principles outline what leadership in the school stands for and aspires to, and what guides leadership development and practice within, across and beyond the school. They provide an overarching view about the purpose of leadership at the school and the way leadership will be enacted.
- A school's leadership vision and principles provide clear statements about how leadership operates within the school, providing clarity for the school and broader community. This also affords an opportunity for school leaders to be held to account for their practice, and a basis from which to improve the quality and impact of leadership.
- A school's leadership vision and principles should be developed in consultation with the school community and key external stakeholders, clearly documented and effectively communicated to the school and broader community.

3. Leadership processes
- Developing agreed leadership processes ensures that there is efficient, effective and consistent leadership practice and decision making within, across and beyond the school. It allows us to understand and manage key relationships and interdependencies within and beyond the leadership ecosystem.
- The processes and systems developed should be applicable to leadership in all areas of the school and, where relevant, should inform and guide leadership processes used beyond the school.

Understanding the relationships between various parts of the school's leadership ecosystem is critical in managing important interrelationships more effectively.
- Leadership processes should be developed in consultation with the school community so that they are aligned with the school's ethos and cultural values, and so they are well understood by all community members.
- Well-documented, understood and applied leadership processes will provide certainty and coherence for leaders and for the school community. Members of the school community may not always agree with the results of a process, but they will understand that matters have been considered in a consistent and comprehensive manner.

4. Leadership focuses
- Establishing the key focuses for the school's leadership effort assists leaders to target and improve their endeavours and provides transparency for the school community about what leadership will be focused on.
- Identifying the key focuses of leadership ensures that the right things get the attention they require and helps concentrate leadership activity on key outcomes and improvements. It is suggested here that 'leadership focuses' should include 2 major areas:
  - school improvement priorities identified by the school through its improvement planning processes
  - improvements to the school's leadership approach.
- It goes without saying that leadership should be investing significant effort on improving school and student outcomes (see Chapters 8 and 9), but if we are to continue to improve how leadership operates at a school then we also need to identify priority leadership focuses. To improve leadership practice and impact we need to be explicit about what we are working on improving.
- In terms of identifying the key areas for leadership focus, it is important that leadership concentrates its efforts on a discrete number of critical areas rather than a broad range of things. There is a tendency in schools to try to do everything. Identifying

specific leadership focuses allows us to sustain and deepen our leadership effort on identified matters of importance, rather than spread effort across a broad range of matters that are unlikely to receive the attention they require for our effort to be as successful as we might wish.

5. Leadership impact
- Leadership impact provides an opportunity to understand, manage and improve the operation and impact of leadership within, across and beyond a school, with a central focus on improved student outcomes.
- Understanding whether your leadership approach is operating effectively, what impact it is having on leadership efficacy across the school and understanding the impact it is (or is not) having on improving school and student outcomes can assist in working out how to improve the school's leadership approach.
- Leadership impact provides a framework for setting, resourcing, developing, measuring and improving leadership performance and impact.

Attributes of ecosystems

As noted in Chapter 1, the 5 ecosystem leadership elements outlined here (see Figure 2.1 on p. 26) were identified and developed by examining the attributes of natural ecosystems. But what are the attributes of natural ecosystems that were identified and how did they inform development of each of the leadership elements?

Here we take a deeper dive into the relationship between natural ecosystems and the ecosystem leadership framework for schools. We examine the form and function of natural ecosystems and how the associated ecosystem leadership elements have been identified and developed.

Table 2.1 on p. 30 shows the relationship between 'natural ecosystems' and 'ecosystem leadership'. It outlines how the natural ecosystem attributes membership, operation and connectivity inform the design of each of the ecosystem leadership elements context, vision, processes, focuses and impact.

Table 2.1 Overview of the relationship between 'natural ecosystems attributes' and 'ecosystem leadership elements'

	Natural ecosystem attributes		
Ecosystem leadership elements	*Membership* – the constituent parts of the system	*Operation* – how the system operates	*Connectivity* – how the system interacts with other systems
Context – the internal and external contexts in which the leadership ecosystem operates	A leadership ecosystem should consider school member needs, interests and aspirations.	Leadership ecosystem operation should be consistent with local and broader needs, interest and aspirations.	A leadership ecosystem should interact with the broader context in which the school operates.
Vision – an overarching view about the purpose of leadership at the school and the way leadership will be enacted	A leadership ecosystem vision and principles should reflect the needs, interest and aspirations of the various members of the school community.	A leadership ecosystem should be clear about the way it will operate to achieve its stated purposes.	The vision and principles of a leadership ecosystem should take account of the school's external environment.
Processes – Leadership processes and systems within, across and beyond the school	A leadership ecosystem's processes should facilitate effective interaction between the members of a school.	Leadership ecosystem processes should ensure that the school's leadership approach works in an integrated and connected manner for the benefit all members of the school.	Leadership ecosystem processes should facilitate effective engagement with the school's external environment.
Focuses – the key focuses of the school's leadership effort	Leadership ecosystem focuses should apply to the work of all school leaders and the school community should be fully aware of the focuses.	A leadership ecosystem should be directly focused on what is important to and for the school, with a strong focus on improving the school's leadership approach, and school and student outcomes.	The leadership focuses of a school may include externally driven influences, e.g. system or community policy, priorities, and/or research
Impact – improving leadership performance and impact	A leadership ecosystem should involve the school community in the development and implementation of leadership impact and improvement measures.	A leadership ecosystem should include processes to measure and improve the effectiveness of the leadership effort.	A leadership ecosystem should effectively manage its engagement with the world beyond the school.

Each of the 3 natural ecosystem attributes are discussed in detail here.

1. Ecosystem membership

Ecosystems can include a broad diversity of species and groups of species[1] that successfully interact with each other within that system and with species in surrounding or associated systems. The species that make up an ecosystem will be based broadly on the climatic and geological conditions or context in which the ecosystem sits. In an ecosystem, there are strong relationships between the members of the ecosystem and how the ecosystem operates, with each influencing the other. The type of species in the ecosystem, their activity and the interrelationships between the member species will influence how the system operates as a whole; and how the system operates will influence the type, activity and interrelationship of each of the member species. Ecosystems are integrated systems that are critically influenced by the membership characteristics of the system.

Schools similarly have rich, diverse and complex membership characteristics, with school members and membership groups interacting in various ways and impacting and influencing each other and the school more broadly, and conversely being influenced by the internal context. A school's membership can include internal members: students, parents, teachers, school leaders and support staff; and external members: local community, business and government groups and individuals, school system representatives, and broader education, community and business sector members. Each of these groups and individuals will have needs, interests and aspirations for the manner in which the school operates and the nature and importance of each group or individual will, of course, vary from school to school. It is important that school leaders understand the 'membership context' in which they operate. As Beatriz Pont notes in her review of the leadership policy reform literature, 'The review findings indicate that leadership practices

---

1 Biology Dictionary (n.d.) *Niche*, accessed 22 September 2020. https://biologydictionary.net/niche/; Vold T and DA Buffett (eds) (2008) *Ecological concepts, principles and applications to conservation*, Bio Diversity BC, accessed 29 July 2022. http://www.biodiversitybc.org > ecological concepts 2008

and the potential impact of leaders is moderated by the context, which can be conducive to change or may not be conducive to change'.[2]

Explicitly considering a school's leadership context helps a school establish a leadership approach that reflects and integrates with the unique circumstances in which the school sits. Better understanding things like the school's historical nature, the needs, interests and aspirations of school members, and their impact on the school's current and future leadership approach, is foundational for the development of a nuanced school leadership ecosystem. This improved understanding of the school's context can be used to inform the development of a leadership vision that reflects the school's distinctive conditions, honours its past and present, and that can drive future improvement in school and student outcomes. A leadership vision and a set of leadership principles (see Chapter 5) ensure that school members have clarity about the core purpose, role and operation of leadership in the school.

Within ecosystems, species can be organised in various ways and have varying levels of organisation,[3] including habitats, communities and populations within and across the different topographical areas or zones of the ecosystem. Within and between species in these groups, there are different processes that operate, including food chains and food webs, energy cycles and water systems.

Schools develop and operate a broad range of leadership processes and systems to manage a variety of school areas, projects, programs and administrative functions. Reviewing our understanding of a school's membership characteristics can assist us to analyse current and future leadership processes within and across a school in a more holistic manner and uncover how consistent and coherent our suite of school leadership processes is. Identifying membership levels of organisation, niches and functional groups, for example, might help us ensure that our leadership approach embeds processes that facilitate effective and efficient interaction between the diversity of school members and membership groups, and improve leadership consistency, coherence and integration.

---

2 Pont (2020:165)
3 Cleland EE (2011) 'Biodiversity and ecosystem stability', *Nature Education Knowledge*, 3(10):14; Sagoff M (2003) 'The plaza and the pendulum: two concepts of ecological science', *Biology & Philosophy*, 18:529–552, https://doi.org/10.1023/A:1025566804906

When Cameron Peverett started as principal at Colac Specialist School in western Victoria, Australia, the first thing he did was to look at the various groups across the school and understand their stated role, their make-up, and how they fit within the school's leadership structure. It was important for him to understand each of the groups' place in the school's leadership 'web' of discussion, consultation, organisation, influence and decision-making. By understanding the current 'lay of the land' he was able to consider what appeared to be working and what was not, and how the school's leadership approach might be improved. He identified that creating a viable and purposeful curriculum was essential for the school and used this as a vehicle for redesigning the way change and improvement across the school could be lead.

Developing an understanding of a school's membership will help ensure that the leadership approach is fit for purpose, consistent, comprehensive and guided by the school's needs, interests and aspirations.

2. Ecosystem operation

There are a range of processes that operate within and across ecosystems to support the viability of the system and the success of its members. There are processes and interactions, such as food webs and food chains, nutrient cycles and the flow of matter and energy through the system to provide ecosystem members with the things they need to survive and develop (as individual species, as groups of species, and to create an integrated and self-sustaining system of support).

Schools develop and operate a range of processes, systems and cycles designed to connect the various members of the school community, and to manage the operation of the school so that it can achieve its prime focus of improving school and student outcomes. Leadership processes and systems typically found in schools include decision-making structures such as curriculum committees, school councils or boards, leadership teams and processes for selecting staff and for positions of responsibility.

The success of an ecosystem is directly related to how well it operates within the context of its local and broader conditions, and its capacity to successfully adjust its operation to meet changes in those conditions as they arise. The design and operation of a leadership ecosystem should account for its leadership context, considering the local and broader context of the school to ensure that leadership operates in a way that acknowledges and meets the needs, interests and aspirations of the school and the broader community.

An ecosystem is also dependent upon the effectiveness of the processes that operate within and across the system, ensuring that the system operates as a connected whole, and that there is consistency of purpose and approach among the processes. A successful leadership system should be clear about what it is attempting to achieve and the way it will operate to achieve its purpose. The development of a school leadership vision and a set of leadership principles (see Chapter 5) provides school leaders with a roadmap for enacting leadership within and beyond the school, informs and guides the other elements of the ecosystem leadership approach (processes, focuses and impact), and provides the school and its broader community with clarity about the overarching 'why' and 'how' of the school's leadership design and operation.

The processes that operate in an ecosystem can vary in several ways: duration, impact, size, complexity, and importantly are often fit for purpose, creating connections and interdependencies that support effective operation of the ecosystem. The leadership processes and systems we develop and use within and across a school need to be cognisant of the need for those processes to support and reinforce high-quality connection between parts of the school and beyond the school and serve to discourage fragmentation between school members and stakeholders. Processes that involve appropriate consultation, that are accessible to all members of the school and that are consistently applied can ensure that the school's leadership approach works in an integrated and connected manner for the benefit all members of the school.

Natural ecosystems operate in ways that ensure that the system benefits its members and the system more broadly; they focus the system's effort on maintaining and developing a healthy and successful system. A school leadership ecosystem should be directly focused on what is important to and for the school. Ecosystem leadership should articulate the 'what' of leadership in the school – a set of clearly defined leadership focuses that will deliver improved leadership, and school and student outcomes. The leadership focuses should be based on the school's leadership vision and principles and inform development and operation of the school's leadership processes and leadership impact.

The relationships between interconnected ecosystems are complex and can vary widely in form, function and impact.

> As mentioned in Chapter 1, a successful leadership system I was involved in as a principal, was a network of local schools. This leadership system included all the local schools: primary and secondary, government, catholic and independent, and its membership included each of the principals and school council presidents. The network planned and implemented shared initiatives, supported each other in various evaluative activities (to gain data on shared successes and challenges), had clear lines of communication and consultation, and an agreed process of governance. The network was successful at attracting extra support and resources for the group of schools.

3. Ecosystem connectivity

While an ecosystem can usually be considered a self-sustaining and autonomous system, an ecosystem's boundaries can be ambiguous and it is likely that there will be significant connection and interaction with surrounding ecosystems, including interaction between the members and processes of each. For example, a plant species may be abundant on the border of both a grassland and an adjacent river ecosystem and consumed by different animals from each of the 2 ecosystems. Interaction between ecosystems does not just include physically adjacent or located ecosystems, it can also include physically distant systems, for example, 2 ecosystems that share a migratory bird species, where breeding in one may be dependent upon their success in seasonal foraging in another.

The broader systems, processes and contexts that schools operate within and interconnect with will vary from school to school, including for example: other schools and networks of schools, government and education system operational processes, policies and priorities; and socio-economic and cultural circumstances.

A school leadership ecosystem needs to understand the nature of its external interconnections in order to ensure productive management of the various inputs into the school (e.g. resourcing, policy requirements, information and data), the school's outputs (e.g. student outcomes, learning from local initiatives and innovations, contributions to local and broader networks) and to understand leadership impact on school and student outcomes and continuously improve leadership performance.

Understanding the nature of the school's broader physical, socio-economic, cultural, policy and historical contexts and ensuring that a leadership approach effectively integrates the needs, interests and aspirations of our school community, with those from key external stakeholders is critical for ensuring that the school can successfully operate within the context in which it exists.

The broad way a school leadership ecosystem operates (its leadership principles – see Chapter 5) should take account of, and integrate with, the school's external environment. Detailing the purpose (leadership vision) and operational principles of a leadership ecosystem ensures that the leadership system's overarching design and operation manages the expectations and requirements of critical external stakeholders.

School leaders are uniquely placed; their roles often include contact with a diverse range of people, teams and organisations, both inside and beyond the school.

> As a school principal, my leadership interactions in any one day, and sometimes in any one hour, could include a mix of individual school staff, students and parents, teams of people from the school, together with staff from the local council, the local community, professional associations and the Department of Education and Training. It was incumbent upon me to ensure that the way I engaged in each of these interactions was consistent with my interpretation of what the school valued, what it was aspiring to achieve and the cultural mores of the school community. I was conscious of representing the school, and making decisions consistent with my interpretations of these things, but on reflection, how consistent was my practice and decision-making with other leaders from the school? There were few instances when we as leaders across the school had explicit conversations about

what underpinned our leadership or came to consistent and agreed positions on how we would lead and make decisions. In retrospect, I suspect that our leadership practice was ad hoc and based on implicit assumptions about how we *would* lead. Developing a more comprehensive and agreed view about the nature, focus and priority of leadership within and beyond the school could have ensured that that we were not leaving our *leadership connectivity* outside the school to chance and assumption.

There will of course from time to time be certain external influences that a school will have no choice about responding to and/or influence over how they are to be integrated into the school's leadership activity. Having a clear understanding of how best to integrate these influences or requirements with our local leadership design and understanding how this integration might affect our leadership design and operation will be critical for ensuring that we meet the needs and interests of the school and that we can improve school and student outcomes.

Developing a leadership ecosystem

Developing a leadership ecosystem that is consistently applied, able to be easily used and understood by all members of the school community and which considers the needs, interest and dispositions of leaders and followers alike is no easy challenge. For many schools it will be a big stretch and for others it may just require a few simple modifications or additions. Understanding what a leadership ecosystem should be like for a particular school will take time and practise and will need to consider a broad range of factors.

Chapter 3 provides advice about how to develop a leadership ecosystem using the framework described in this chapter.

CHAPTER 3
Building an ecosystem leadership approach

Based on our new learnings about the elements of the ecosystem leadership framework and the attributes of natural ecosystems, what should an ecosystem leadership approach include? Who should it apply to, how will it fit with other forms or approaches to leadership, and how will it relate to the school and its context?

It is important to consider the sort of things that might be significant in designing a more integrated system of leadership to ensure that the approach is comprehensive, fit for purpose and is able to be adjusted and improved over time. Being explicit about who the approach applies to, how it will be developed and how it is to be enacted are key foundations for the successful development of an ecosystem leadership approach. It will ensure clarity and coherence of the approach and buy-in from the school community.

In this chapter we will briefly explore the development and implementation of an ecosystem leadership approach and introduce a series of steps that can be used to guide development of the approach.

School leadership ecosystem considerations

Leadership within, across and beyond a school

A well-functioning ecosystem includes effective and efficient processes and interactions between the component parts in and across the system, as well as beyond the ecosystem with adjacent systems that impact on the ecosystem, including the broader biome or context in which the ecosystem exists.

The approach outlined in this book makes explicit reference to leadership 'within', 'across' and 'beyond' a school. By creating an approach that includes all leadership practice at and beyond the school, we provide the leaders of that school with a comprehensive framework to guide their leadership effort. For followers and external players, we demonstrate leadership practice that is consistent and aligned with the school's ethos and leadership design.

This ecosystem leadership approach is based on the idea that an effective school-wide leadership approach will be comprehensive, consistent and interconnected. The approach applies to all leadership activity at and beyond the school and all of the school's leadership practice occurs within the agreed parameters set by the school. By ensuring this, we lay strong foundations on which to create consistent leadership practice that ensures coherence and transparency in leadership application for all internal and external stakeholders.

Leadership approach

If we are to create a leadership approach that can be explicitly followed by all leaders at the school and understood by stakeholders within and beyond the school, then we need to be intentional in the way in which we create, communicate and implement our leadership approach.

This book refers to both leadership 'design' and 'practice'. Creating and documenting a leadership design assists us to implement more effectively, monitor, evaluate and improve leadership practice at the school, and, over time, to improve that leadership design.

We need a leadership design that is explicit and clear to the school community and can be communicated to external stakeholders – a design that spells out what leadership at the school stands for and how it will operate across the school. The design needs to be developed through extensive consultation so that it honours the historical context, traditions, aspirations and ethos of the school community and the contexts in which the school exists, and is broadly owned by all school stakeholders.

Developing a leadership ecosystem design provides school leaders and schools with:

- clear and explicit information about how leadership is to operate within and beyond the school
- a framework to lead both individuals and teams collectively
- information about how school leadership processes will be developed, operated and managed

- a framework for leadership development and capacity building within the school
- guidance for new staff within a school, ensuring greater continuity and consistency of leadership practice and follower understanding of the leadership approach.

A leadership design also allows the school to hold leaders to account for how their individual and collective school leadership practice is operationalised both within and beyond the school.

Individual and collective school leadership

An ecosystem is inclusive of the diverse range of elements, processes and interactions within and beyond that system. An ecosystem can include elements that are small and apply to specific areas of the ecosystem, those that are large and may take up areas or apply across the whole system, and parts that are in between. These parts can be quite different in nature, purpose and operation, but are connected so that all parts contribute to the health and effectiveness of the total system.

This book advocates an approach in which leadership can be of varying orders of magnitude, diversity of structure and operation so long as they are integrated into and consistent with other elements and processes and contribute positively to the broader system.

The approach detailed in this book does not mandate a particular 'style' of leadership or suggest that leaders should all lead in the same way. Rather, the approach suggests that there needs to be an integration of the key leadership elements in a school to ensure that leadership is not working against itself, and that there are processes and structures that foster consistency and coherence of practice. It is worth for example, a school investing time in helping school leaders understand their preferred style of leadership and for school leaders to be cognisant of the style preferences of others with whom they lead. While leaders will need to adjust their preferences to the school's agreed approach (including adhering to *leadership vision* and *processes*), it is always helpful for leaders to understand the nature of their leadership colleagues' preferred ways of leading. Chapter 5 discusses the value of better understanding our fellow leaders.

An ecosystem approach applies to all leadership activity. When ecosystems contain things that do not work, such as invasive species, or parts that are out of alignment (think plague or over-population), the effective functioning of the ecosystem is compromised. If we have aspects of leadership in a school that are not working as well other aspects, then disharmony and dysfunction is likely to occur. The leadership approach must apply to individual and collective school leadership activity, including formal and informal leadership, and leaders at all levels of the school.

Creating change in a school can be a challenge; many schools and school systems have been the subject of a great deal of reform over many years and there are naturally varying degrees of change fatigue in schools based on this and other local influences and experience. This of course does not mean that we should not undertake further change or reform, but as we all know, we need to plan for and carefully manage change based on the school's previous experiences and current circumstances and on what is most likely to lead to successful change in that school.

Implementing an ecosystem approach to school leadership

School leaders are increasingly aware of the need for project planning and implementation that is strategic, comprehensive, inclusive and based on best available research and data. A great leadership design is only as a good as the effectiveness of its implementation. Developing a clear plan to operationalise the school's design and to successfully manage any change is critical for ensuring the success of an ecosystem leadership approach in a school.

There are a range of critical overarching conditions and practices that are worth considering when developing and implementing the various elements of this approach to leadership. While much of this is considered good change management practice for the implementation of any new process or procedure, it is worth considering what practices, techniques and processes will assist in maximising the chances of success. Potential design and implementation risks need to be managed, and the design and implementation approach must be consistent with the school's internal and external nature, conditions and context.

Project management implementation

There is a large body of literature about effective project management, including several detailed methodologies and approaches. Some common styles include Agile, Scrum and Kanban practices; waterfall or PRINCE2.[1] These approaches are discussed further in Chapter 9.

While many project management methodologies use similar design and implementation steps, strategies and approaches, it is suggested here that schools should consider the following key principles when developing their leadership ecosystem:

- use of best evidence and data
- effective stakeholder engagement
- clear and consistent communication
- a planned, documented and strategic approach
- comprehensive evaluative processes
- agile and flexible design and implementation
- ensure students are at the centre of the design and implementation.

Further discussion and information about project and change management design and implementation, including the principles outlined here, are explored in subsequent chapters as we examine each element of the ecosystem. Chapter 9 explores options for undertaking a comprehensive approach to developing and implementing a whole-school leadership ecosystem. If you have little experience with approaches to project management, it may be worth investing some time learning more about the important elements of effective project management, together with an understanding of how to select an approach, or elements of an approach, that will suit your school's needs and interests.

---

1 nutcache (n.d.) '8 top project management methods, approaches, techniques', *nutcache blog*, accessed 15 September 2020. https://www.nutcache.com/blog/8-top-project-management-approaches-methods-techniques/

Steps for building a leadership ecosystem

The approach outlined in this book builds a school's leadership ecosystem through a systematic process of activity focused on each of the ecosystem leadership elements (see Figure 3.1).

Step 1 'context' involves a comprehensive analysis of the school's context and the development of an understanding of the implications of that context for leadership at the school.

This understanding of the school's context is then used to develop Step 2 'vision', together with a set of principles to guide leadership practice at the school.

Step 3 'processes' is for schools to consider the current range of *leadership processes* used within, across and beyond the school. This may involve adapting current processes and/or developing new ones that are consistent with Steps 1 and 2.

Step 4 'focuses' decides the main focuses for leadership at the school; the development of a discrete set of high-impact priorities that are most likely to improve school and student outcomes in that school (see

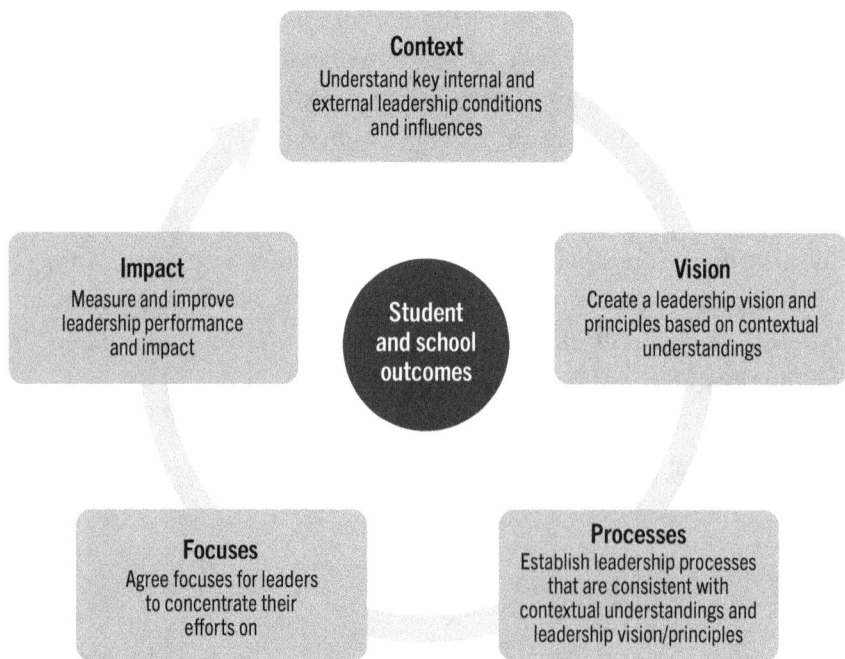

Figure 3.1 Steps for developing the ecosystem leadership elements

Chapters 8 and 9). It is likely that the work undertaken in the previous steps will provide significant data for this step.

Step 5 'impact' understands how leadership performance can be measured and evaluated, to provide evidence and focus for improving leadership performance. This can include adjustments to Steps 2, 3 and 4, creating an integrated system of leadership that is self-improving, agile, coherent and that improves school and student outcomes.

While many schools will have undertaken some or all the activities suggested in this book, the processes outlined provide ideas that could assist schools to further improve or refine their leadership design and practice. Most importantly, the process outlined here provides an opportunity for schools to consider how integrated their leadership practice is and to use the ideas in this book to create a deliberate, consistent and comprehensive approach to leadership.

The subsequent chapters of this book examine the individual elements of an ecosystem approach to school leadership: context, vision, processes, focuses and impact.

Chapters 4 to 8 explore the characteristics of the elements, provide guidance about how to develop and implement that aspect of the approach, and explore examples of effective practice found in a range of schools.

Chapter 9 explores ways of designing and implementing an ecosystem approach to leadership across a school, including project and change management approaches and strategies.

CHAPTER 4
Leadership context

Leadership context — the internal and external nature and circumstances of the ecosystem.

Understanding internal and external school circumstances to create the foundations of a leadership approach that is aligned with the needs, interests and aspirations of a school community.

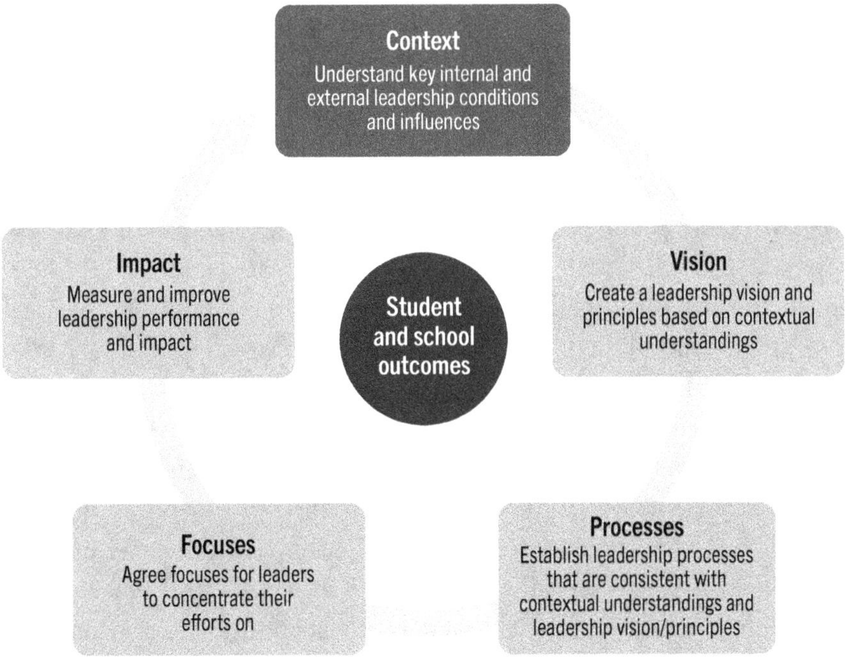

Context
Understand key internal and external leadership conditions and influences

Impact
Measure and improve leadership performance and impact

Student and school outcomes

Vision
Create a leadership vision and principles based on contextual understandings

Focuses
Agree focuses for leaders to concentrate their efforts on

Processes
Establish leadership processes that are consistent with contextual understandings and leadership vision/principles

Figure 4.1 Leadership context

The way we live our lives is intricately connected to the world around us. We make use of transport, food and health services to travel, eat and stay healthy; we meet with family, friends and colleagues to interact socially; and we participate in adventure, art and sporting events for fitness and entertainment. We are creatures of our environment, influenced by and influencing the 'context' in which we live. There is a complex interplay between us and our environment, a two-way street of influence and impact. While each of the interconnections we have will vary in terms of scale, duration and importance, and be unique for everyone, we are inextricably connected.

Clearly, the context in which we operate matters. To ignore it, or to take little account of the world around us will have implications for how well we live, survive and thrive within that context, and will have consequences of varying degrees for our communities and environments.

My working life has been one of change and diversity across the education sector. I have taught in primary and secondary schools, at the Melbourne Zoo and in juvenile justice. I have worked in policy and procurement units, and I have been the director of an education leadership institute. I have loved all my roles and disliked them in equal measure at various times. I have been bored and challenged and annoyed and frustrated; sometimes all in one day! Of course, each organisation and each unit or team I worked in was different (as they are for most of us) and required me to adjust the way I led. But did I adjust adequately to each context? Did I adjust daily, weekly, monthly? Did I adjust because I was made to, because I wanted to or because I needed to? Was I a good fit for all the leadership tasks or roles I undertook? Was I appointed to those roles because of my 'fit'?

Context is a complex area of consideration; as leaders we ignore it at our peril. Leadership that does not account for the circumstances of an organisation's internal and external conditions risks operating in ways that neglect opportunities to maximum its impact, or worse, operate in opposition to the prevailing conditions that exist. To use a natural ecosystem analogy, leadership that does not account for its context risks being 'like a fish out of water'.

Natural ecosystems are not just connected to the elements within and around them, they are an integral part of that collection of elements. They exist within, together, and because of their connection with the world around them; they are a critical part of the system in which they exist. An ecosystem's context will impact on the way an ecosystem operates, with the success of the ecosystem determined by how well it interacts with its local and broader context.

In Chapters 1 and 2 of this book, we considered how we might use what we know about natural ecosystems to create a more systematic, comprehensive and intentional approach to leadership in our schools, and we identified several elements that could assist with this endeavour, including leadership context. Considering the context in which we lead is foundational for establishing a strong leadership ecosystem in a school.

Schools operate across and within the full range of a society's social, political and geographic environments. Schools exist in the remotest areas of the world, in the most crowded cities, in areas of wealth and poverty, in areas of peace and areas of war. Every school is different, and every school reflects the context in which it operates. The degree to which a school makes use of its context to improve the school and student outcomes will vary (see Chapters 8 and 9); harnessing this in better ways can have great benefits for a school, its community and for society more broadly. Kenneth Leithwood and colleagues show that 'Recent research has highlighted the importance of leaders being responsive to context and highlighted how effective school leaders understand and respond appropriately to the different contextual demands that they face.'[1]

Effective use of school context in leadership is not, however, just a matter of school leaders responding to the context in which they lead; it is far more complex than that. Leaders and their context impact on each other. There is significant interplay between a leader's context, the way school leaders operate within that context, and the impact of the leader's practices on that context. Figure 4.2 on p. 52 outlines the relationship inherent in the leader/context relationship. As Leithwood and colleagues suggest, 'The ways in which leaders apply ... basic leadership practices

---

1   Leithwood K, Harris A and Hopkins D (2019:5) 'Seven strong claims about successful school leadership revisited', *School Leadership & Management*, 40(1):5–22, doi:10.1080/13632434.2019.1596077

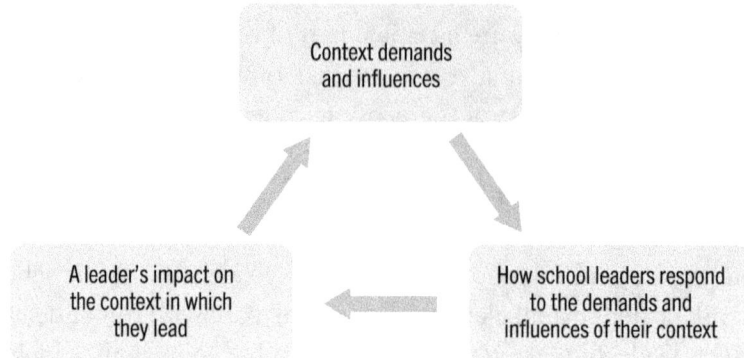

Figure 4.2 The relationship between school leaders and their context

– not the practices themselves – demonstrate responsiveness to, rather than dictation by, the contexts in which they work.'²

Why context is important for school leadership

We live in a constantly changing and dynamic world; in 2013 David Shilling suggested that '… on average human knowledge is doubling every 13 months. According to IBM, the build out of the "internet of things" will lead to the doubling of knowledge every 12 hours.'³ It is hard now to imagine living without a mobile phone, without being able to travel long distances by car or forms of public transport, or without interacting with the world through the internet. Our context is constantly changing, and in many ways, we change with it.

There is increasing discussion about the place of context in 'leadership theory and practice'. This includes the notion of 'contingency theory', which Jesmin Islam and Hui Hu suggest in its broadest sense is '… an approach to the study of organizational behaviour in which explanations are given as to how contingent factors such as technology, culture and the external environment influence the design and function of

---

2   Leithwood et al. (2019:5)
3   Schilling DR (2013) 'Knowledge doubling every 12 months, soon to be every 12 hours', *Industry Tap Into News*, accessed 25 November 2020. https://www.industrytap.com/knowledge-doubling-every-12-months-soon-to-be-every-12-hours/3950

organizations.'4 Contingency theory suggests that a leader's effectiveness is contingent on whether their leadership style suits a particular situation. According to this theory, an individual can be an effective leader in one circumstance and an ineffective leader in another.[5]

The contingency theory of leadership includes discussion about how an organisation's circumstances can be used to ensure that leadership design and effort is maximised. There are so many variables in a workplace that can impact on how successful a leader is, with that success contingent upon (among other things) the interplay between those variables and a person's leadership style. Adjusting the organisation in some way, or adjusting the way in which leaders lead, can result in different outcomes.

There is also broad discussion about the aspects of context that leadership should account for. William Alexander and colleagues argue that 'For the senior-most leaders in an organization, especially the CEO, the context includes the external business environment, strategy, culture, organizational complexity and stakeholder expectations.'[6] While it might be that these contexts are not relevant to every organisation, and there may be particular contexts not mentioned here that are important to some and not others, it is critical to note that an organisation's leadership approach and the requirements for successful leadership will vary between organisations based on their context.

So, do we just select leaders that will 'fit' a certain circumstance; leaders that are likely to be successful in a particular context? That would be a complex task, one that would require a strong methodology for determining exactly the particular circumstances of that organisation, anticipating variations to circumstances over time, and implementing a precise selection process to decide on the most suitable candidate. Further, such an approach is unlikely to meet the needs of an

---

4   Islam J and Hu H (2012:5159) 'A review of literature on contingency theory in managerial accounting', *African Journal of Business Management*, 6(15):5159–5164
5   Indeed Career Guide (2020) *Understanding the contingency theory of leadership*, Indeed.com, accessed 20 November 2020. https://www.indeed.com/career-advice/career-development/contingency-theory-of-leadership; Alexander W, Anderson M, Anterasian C and Lee J (2017) *Context matters: the five elements of context that most impact senior leader success*, SpencerStuart, accessed 9 June 2021. https://www.spencerstuart.com; Groysberg B, McLean A and Nohria N (May 2006) 'Are leaders portable?' *Harvard Business Review*
6   Alexander et al. (2017:2)

organisation as its context changes and is unlikely to create a leadership approach that is dynamic and able to adjust to meet evolving needs and unforeseen changes in an organisation's interests and aspirations.

Perhaps the alternative is to take an approach to leadership in which leaders adjust their 'style' and effort to fit their circumstances. This is something that I am sure we all do to varying degrees in our schools. In the leadership literature this is known as the Situational Leadership Model, which argues that leaders should '… adapt their leadership styles to fit their team members and their individual abilities. This model believes that leaders should first consider the variables that affect their workplace and then decide the best tactic for how to proceed.'[7] The effectiveness of this is of course contingent upon a leader's capacity to adjust. It relies on their personal and professional capacity to use their skills, knowledge and experience and to change their practice and perhaps their disposition or attitudes, together with the organisation's capacity to facilitate and support that change. Leithwood and colleagues describe the potential importance of a leader's 'personal leadership resources', suggesting that 'While further research is required, a well-defined set of cognitive, social and psychological "personal leadership resources" show promise of explaining a high proportion of variation in the practices enacted by school leaders.'[8]

At a broader level, there is evidence that the effectiveness of school leadership can be dependent upon on the school's external context. Pont argues that 'leadership practices and the potential impact of leaders is moderated by the context, which can be conducive to change or may not be conducive to change.'[9]

Our challenge is to better understand our *individual and collective* leadership context and use that understanding to improve our leadership practice and approach to improve school and student outcomes. The individual context of our school and its leadership should serve as a firm basis to inform the development of a leadership ecosystem.

---

7   Indeed Editorial Team (2022) *Contingency theory of leadership: definition and models*, Indeed.com, accessed 28 July 2022. https://www.indeed.com/career-advice/career-development/contingency-theory-of-leadership
8   Leithwood et al. (2019:11)
9   Pont (2020:165)

In this chapter we will consider 4 key aspects of leadership context:

1. Understand individual and collective school leadership context.
2. Identify critical elements of a leader's context.
3. Use context to improve outcomes.
4. Create the foundations of a leadership ecosystem.

1. Understand individual and collective school leadership context

Context for school leaders can include a broad range of factors, including economic, political and sociocultural contexts,[10] as well as school system characteristics, such as '… the level of decentralisation; the extent of school autonomy; the quality of teaching professionals; the way teachers are assigned to schools; and incentives for collaborative cultures.'[11]

If I think about what was important for me as a school leader in terms of context, my list would include both internal and external school elements. 'Internal contexts' included the school's history, staff circumstances (individual and collective), staffing profile, financial circumstances and resources, infrastructure, student and family socio-economic and cultural demographic information, performance data and the school's strategic plan (and previous planning and development activity and performance).

'External contexts' included funding and resource provision, government and education system policy, priorities and initiatives, the education sector (local, national and international), the business sector (including local businesses and broader business policy and narrative), the local and regional networks of schools, the principal and teacher professional and industrial organisations (and their services, policies and initiatives), the local council, community service organisations, local businesses and community groups.

---

10 Hallinger P (2018) 'Bringing context out of the shadows of leadership', *Educational Management Administration & Leadership*, 46(1):5–24, doi.org/10.1177/1741143216670652
11 Pont (2020:166)

Annette Braun and colleagues describe 4 contextual dimensions that can impact policy enactment in schools:

1. Situated contexts (e.g. locale, school histories, intakes and settings).
2. Professional contexts (e.g. values, teacher commitments and experiences, and policy management in schools).
3. Material contexts (e.g. staffing, budget, buildings, technology and infrastructure).
4. External contexts (e.g. degree and quality of local authority support, pressures and expectations from broader policy context, such as Ofsted ratings, league table positions, legal requirements and responsibilities).[12]

Phillip Hallinger suggests that '… there is a growing consensus that there exists a generic set of leadership practices (e.g. goal setting, developing people) which must be adapted to meet the needs and constraints that describe different school contexts. However, to date, researchers have yet to develop a theory or report comprehensive findings on this challenge.'[13] He examines how different school contexts shape leadership practice, suggesting that the broad categories of school context include: institutional, community, sociocultural, political, economic and school improvement contexts.

A school's 'improvement context' is important to consider as you develop a leadership ecosystem. Schools generally spend a lot of time and effort developing strategic plans and enacting those plans, together with other improvement plans, tactics, initiatives and practices. A leadership ecosystem should ensure that it is aligned with, focused on, and positioned to successfully lead the school's improvement effort. It is not sufficient, however, for a leadership approach to simply adopt the priorities, goals and vision of the school's strategic plan. While focused on improving school performance and delivering the school's strategic

---

12 Braun A, Ball S, Maguire M and Hoskins K (2011:588) 'Taking context seriously: towards explaining policy enactments in the secondary school', *Discourse: Studies in the Cultural Politics of Education* 32(4):585–596
13 Hallinger (2018:5)

plan, a leadership ecosystem needs to understand the *leadership context* it operates in, establish its own *leadership vision* and principles, *processes* and *focuses* and understand its *impact*.

A school leader's context will vary depending upon a leader's role within the school, the shared contexts of the 'leadership collective' at the school, and in terms of each leader's individual context, including '… job knowledge, skills, attitudes and experience a leader brings to the job. The leader's life experience and personal resources act as a prism through which information, problems, opportunities and situations are filtered and interpreted …'[14] The Principal Performance Improvement Tool developed by ACER suggests that 'How a principal works and what they are able to do usually depends on contextual factors including: how long they have been a principal, how long they have been in the current school, the context in which the school operates and internal school factors.'[15] In examining leadership context in schools, it is important to consider both individual and collective leadership contexts, as these will vary depending upon the role, function and circumstances of the individual leader and for various groups or teams of leaders.

Individual leadership context

Understanding and leading in context can contribute to expedient, fit-for-purpose leadership by individual leaders within, across and beyond a school. This is particularly the case when leaders are more aware of the way they lead, their personal leadership skills, knowledge and dispositions and their leadership practice in action. Leaders who have a more nuanced understanding of the context in which they lead will be more confident about their decision-making and interactions as a leader and make decisions that fit better with the circumstances[16] in which they lead.

---

14 Hallinger (2018:7)
15 ACER (Australian Council for Educational Research) (2018b:1) *Principal performance improvement tool*, accessed 16 February 2022. https://research.acer.edu.au/cgi/viewcontent.cgi?article=1032&context=tll_misc
16 Rowley C and Changeboard Team (2016) *Leadership and the importance of context*, Changeboard, accessed 4 August 2022. https://www.changeboard.com/article-details/15535/leadership-and-the-importance-of-context/; Alexander et al. (2017)

A leader needs to understand and account for their own personal context, including their biases,[17] their preferred style of leadership, their leadership strengths and challenges[18] and the relationship between those individual circumstances and their immediate and broader contexts.

> Mary Hutchison is an experienced principal who has led in several schools in Australia. When reflecting on her leadership over many years she found that she had significantly altered her approach over those years. While experience was a great teacher and her leadership altered as she learnt and grew, her leadership approach adjusted significantly based on who, where and what she was leading.
>
> Most of us are aware of needing to fit our leadership to the context we lead in, but how much time do we spend really analysing our leadership approach in terms of our context, and understanding the interplay between ourselves, our leadership and our context?

To develop a better understanding of your individual school leadership context you may like to spend some time considering what your context consists of and the relationships that exist between you and the various elements of that context by working through Activity 1.

Throughout this book you will find 16 activities like Activity 1. These activities have been designed to assist school leaders to develop a better understanding of their leadership (both individual and collective) and to build the foundations for a comprehensive and integrated leadership ecosystem at their school. It is important to note that these activities are suggestions only, and that you may like to modify them to suit your individual circumstances, create different activities or processes, or source activities that others have developed. It is likely that you have already undertaken some of the activities suggested in this book and can use that information as you develop your leadership ecosystem. The collection of 16 activities will result in an 'overview document' that is

---

17 Rowley (2016)
18 Indeed Career Guide (2020)

> **Activity 1: Mapping your individual school leadership context**

Note: This activity could be done by both formal and informal leaders across the school.

Purpose: To assist you to better understand your individual school leadership context.

ACTIVITY

Step 1: List the key elements of your individual leadership context under these 4 contextual dimensions. Create a table to record this information:

1. Situated contexts (e.g. locale, school histories, intakes and settings).
2. Professional contexts (e.g. values, teacher commitments and experiences, and policy management in schools) including the school's improvement approach (e.g. critical elements of the school's strategic plan, and any available leadership performance or opinion survey data).
3. Material contexts (e.g. staffing, budget, buildings, technology and infrastructure).
4. External contexts (e.g. degree and quality of local authority support, pressures and expectations from broader policy context, such as ratings, league table positions, legal requirements and responsibilities).*

Step 2: Use a visual context map (see Figure 4.3 on p. 60 as an example) to show the relationships and interconnections between each of the key elements of your individual leadership context

Step 3: Briefly detail your leadership style and experience:

- *Leadership experience*: outline your formal and informal leadership roles and experiences.
- *Leadership style or preferences*: note the results of any leadership 'style' or 'preference' instruments you have completed.
- *Leadership learning*: detail recent formal and informal learning.
- *Leadership strengths*: note when you are at your best when you are leading. What are you good at (in terms of leadership)?
- *Leadership challenges*: consider how your leadership could improve. What could you do better as a leader?
- *Other*: add your own element/s.

Step 4: Use the information from Step 3 to note where your leadership style is likely to impact on the various elements of the context map identified in Step 2.

Continued ▶

---

* Braun A, Ball S, Maguire M and Hoskins K (2011:588) 'Taking context seriously: towards explaining policy enactments in the secondary school', *Discourse: Studies in the Cultural Politics of Education* 32(4):585–596

My leadership context (assistant principal)

Professional context	Situated context	External context	Material context
School strategic plan	School fundraising committee	School council	Building program
Senior leadership team	Local area demographics	Assistant principal network	Human resources operations
Leadership data	Parents and friends association	Government priorities	School and program budgets
Professional context	School demographic profile		Maintenance program
Curriculum committee	Situated context		
Student welfare program			

Professional context: School strategic plan, Senior leadership team, Leadership data, Curriculum committee, Student welfare program, Parents

Situated context: School fundraising committee, Local area demographics, Parents and friends association, School demographic profile

External context: Government priorities, Assistant Principal network, School council

Material context: Maintenance program, School and program budget, Human resource operations, Building program

Central node: My leadership context (Assistant Principal)

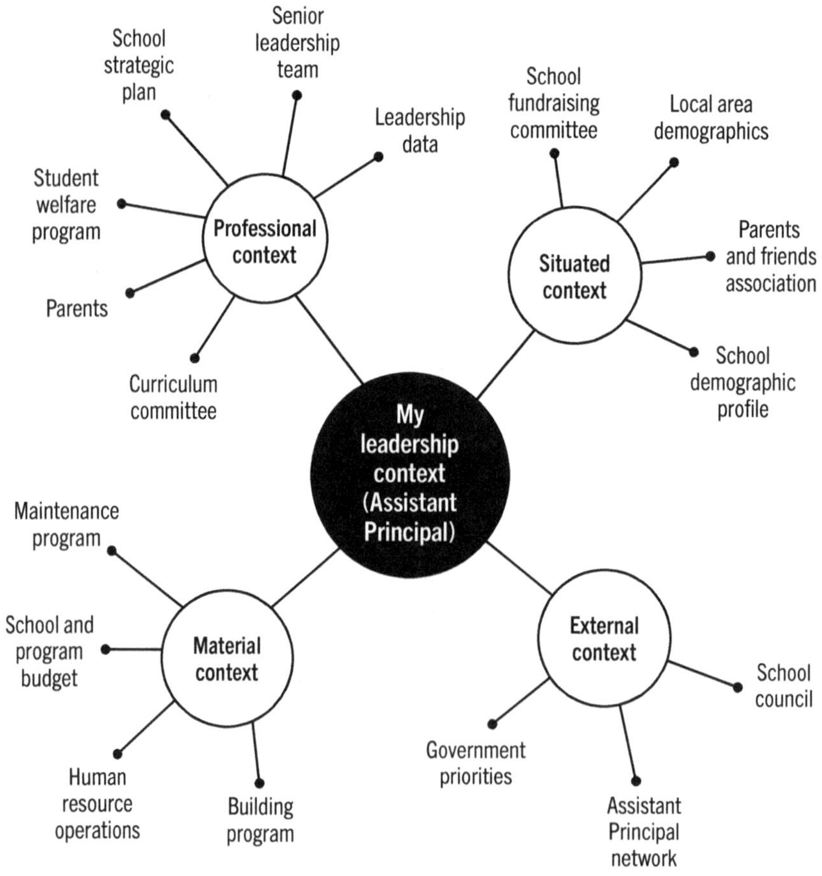

Figure 4.3 Individual context map example

a consolidated set of information about your own ecosystem leadership approach. It will outline your leadership context, vision, principles, processes, focuses and how leadership performance and impact are used to build your leadership ecosystem.

The critical point that is made throughout this book is that there are important elements of a leadership ecosystem that require explicit and intentional development to create a more integrated and comprehensive approach to leadership in your school. Working through the suggested activities and modifying them to suit your need, or creating your own, will help you build an approach that suits the context in which you lead.

Collective leadership context

There is increasing research and evidence about the effectiveness of collective leadership approaches.[19] Recent studies have shown that collective or shared leadership can predict team effectiveness,[20] and lead to higher rates of leader engagement, commitment, leader-to-leader feedback, capacity to meet business challenges, and improved cultures and practice of professional learning, together with a lessened risk of leaders leaving an organisation.[21] In terms of the impact of collective leadership in schools, Seashore and colleagues found that 'Collective leadership has a stronger influence on student achievement than individual leadership.'[22]

A colleague of mine once said to me that they admired my ability to delegate to others; to give leaders in my team the time and space to lead within their area of responsibility, with little interference from me. My initial response was that I was just inherently lazy; that I was happy for them to do the work if it meant that I didn't have to. I was joking, of course, and I went on to say that ultimately it came down to trust; my trust in them to get the job done based on my experiences with them, and trust in myself that I had made a correct assessment of their capabilities and dispositions and was therefore willing to release authority.

---

19 Hmieleski et al. (2012)
20 West et al. (2015)
21 Canwell et al. (2018:19)
22 Seashore et al. (2010:19)

When we work with others, it provides us with opportunities to share our knowledge and understandings about the context we work in, to discuss how best to lead in that context, to reflect on how well we are leading, and to consider how to adjust our planning and decision-making to best meet the needs and interests of our stakeholders.

If we are to work together more effectively as school leaders, we need to have a clearer understanding of our collective context so that we can ensure that our leadership within and across the school is consistent and fit for purpose. Activity 2 has been developed to assist you to share your individual leadership context (Activity 1) with groups or teams of leaders and to develop a more comprehensive understanding of the collective leadership context for that team or group across the school. This activity could be done with the school's leadership team and/or with leaders (both formal and informal) across the school once they have completed Activity 1.

2. Identify critical elements of a leader's context

Some of the elements of the school's context will be more important than others, particularly with respect to the needs, interests, performance and aspirations of the school. Understanding which elements to concentrate effort on is critical in school leadership and will be dependent upon the circumstances of a leader or leadership group, including for example: a leader's/leadership group's role and mandate, the needs of the school community, the structure of the education system, and the school's staffing profile, resources and demographics.

Changes in context may dictate changes to your leadership focus. For example, you may be new to a school, role or leadership group; there may be changes to the leadership staff or structure, in education policy or government strategy, or in a school's performance data. When circumstances change, the things that you focus on and how you enact your leadership may also need to change.

Activity 2: Mapping your collective school leadership context

Purpose: To assist your leadership team or group to better understand your collective school leadership context and to provide information for 'Activity 3: Identifying school leadership context priorities'.

ACTIVITY

Step 1: Share and discuss as a leadership group the team's results from 'Activity 1: Mapping your leadership context'. You may wish to use a protocol like the Ladder of Inference* to guide the discussion.

Step 2: Create a collective view of your shared context using the information from each participant's individual context map (see Figure 4.3 on p. 60), keeping the elements that are relevant to the group, removing those that are not shared by the group and adding any new context elements identified during the discussion. Create a table to record your information; adding extra rows as required and removing the contextual dimension headers if they are no longer required for your deliberations. An example is provided in Figure 4.4.

Context element	Description	Members	Overview
Situated contexts			
Professional contexts			
Material contexts			
External contexts			

Figure 4.4 Collective context elements

---

* Mulder P (2018) *Ladder of Inference*, ToolsHero, accessed 2 June 2021. https://www.toolshero.com/decision-making/ladder-of-inference/

> Rita Singh is the Director of the Indirapuram Group of Institutions based in Delhi, India. Originally, she was principal of one of the schools in the group. When she moved into the director's role with responsibility for all the institutions in the group her leadership context changed. While still a part of the executive leadership team, her new position meant she now had a different relationship with her principal colleagues and the manner of interaction with them changed. Her broader group responsibilities meant that her organisation accountabilities changed, and the breadth of her role across 9 institutions changed her external context. Rita needed to change the nature and focus of her leadership to respond to her changed context.

Deciding which elements of your context should be yours, or your leadership group's priorities, is likely to be a complex task. Identifying the contextual elements that you should concentrate your leadership on may include things like the 'loud voice' or the 'squeaky wheel' (particularly if they have potential to derail school improvement efforts or leadership impact), school performance deficits, quick wins, or things that you can actually make a difference with or successfully influence. Most importantly, the basis of any decision about priorities should be on those elements of the school's leadership context that will impact on improved school and student outcomes.

Activity 3 will assist in prioritising your efforts to improve school and/or student outcomes, and will help to clarify which elements you and your leadership group, and other leaders across the school, should implement. Completing this activity will also assist with the development of a leadership vision and associated principles, and leadership focuses, which are discussed in Chapters 5 and 7.

Activity 3: Identifying school leadership context priorities

Purpose: To assist in the development of individual and/or collective school leadership context priorities.

ACTIVITY

Individual

Step 1: Using the information from 'Activity 1: Mapping your individual leadership context', identify leadership context areas that require focus to improve school and student outcomes.

Step 2: Decide on a priority with the key consideration being the elements that are likely to have the greatest impact on improving school and student outcomes.

Collective

Step 1: Using the table developed in 'Activity 2: Mapping your collective school leadership context', discuss the nature of each of the elements so that there is a shared view.

Step 2: Everyone in the group should list the elements in their preferred priority with the key consideration being the elements that are likely to have the greatest impact on improving school and student outcomes.

Step 3: Collectively share and discuss the group's information from Step 2 with members of your leadership group. You may wish to use a protocol like the Ladder of Inference* to guide the discussion.

Step 4: As a collective, establish on a priority for the leadership context elements. Improving school and student outcomes should be the key metric in the decision making on the order.

---

* Mulder P (2018) *Ladder of Inference*, ToolsHero, accessed 2 June 2021. https://www.toolshero.com/decision-making/ladder-of-inference/

3. Use context knowledge to improve outcomes

Using school leadership context knowledge to improve school and student outcomes requires a comprehensive and intimate understanding of a school's context, so you can identify and adjust the leadership practices that will make the differences you are seeking. It requires careful and effective management of those adjustments to ensure broad school community support and engagement with the changes.

Once you have identified areas of your leadership context that you should prioritise in order to improve school and/or student outcomes the challenge becomes identifying elements of your leadership practice that can assist with this improvement. Leithwood and colleagues argue, '… leadership success in most school contexts requires locally sensitive adaptations of a set of core leadership practices that are generally effective in most circumstances.'[23] They cite 18 core leadership practices that fall under 4 elements:

1. Set directions.
2. Build relationships and develop people.
3. Develop the organisation to support desired practices.
4. Improve the instructional program.[24]

These leadership practices may be worth considering in terms of understanding which of your own practices may need to adjust to successfully focus attention on your identified leadership context priorities.

It is one thing to identify context priorities and associated adjustments to leadership practice, and another to implement those changes. Managing change requires skill and expertise if it is to be done effectively, and when considering changes, such as these, it might be worth thinking about the:

---

[23] Singh SB (2019:563) 'Book review: How school leaders contribute to student success: the four paths framework', *School Leadership & Management*, 39(5):561–564, doi:10.1080/13632434.2018.1523143

[24] Leithwood K, Sun J and Schumacker R (2020) 'How school leadership influences student learning: a test of "the four paths model"', *Educational Administration Quarterly*, 56(4):570–599, doi:10.1177/0013161X19878772

- *nature of the change*: What exactly needs to change and is it within your power to make that change?
- *extent of the change*: How much needs to change?
- *timing of the change*: When and for how long?

The following example illustrates how school leaders often go about this seemingly complex task of leading change in response to their context.

The problem: when I took up my first principal appointment, it was the final 3 months of the school year and, among other things, the staff were working through student grade placements for the next school year. As school leaders know, this can be a pretty complex activity; trying to get a balance in each class of productive friendships groups (a gender balance, an ability balance), matching particular students with teachers who will be able to get the best out of each child, and so forth. The parent expectation in the school for many years had been that they could change a child's allocated class by meeting with the principal once the class lists had been published. Parents were not required to have substantial reasons for the change of class; it was often just choice based on who parents perceived as the 'best' teacher at that year level. If a child was moved, and they usually were, it often created problems of balance in the class that the child was leaving as well as the one they were going to, which undid many hours of careful planning and consideration by the staff.

The challenge: it was clear that a 'change in process' was required, but the change needed to be made in the context of the school's history and cultural expectations regarding this sensitive issue. It needed to honour and balance the needs, interests and expectations of the parents, students and staff, and most importantly result in class composition that would ensure effective student learning for all students.

The change: I did not consciously go through the 3 considerations described in the bulleted list above (nature, extent and timing of the change), but in practice it did run along those lines. Working with the

Continued ▶

> school's senior leadership team and year-level leaders we developed a new decision-making process that flipped the nature and timing of student and parent input. We sought their input prior to creating new class lists, and we were explicit about the extent of the input that was required and would be considered as a part of the decision-making process (information about the child's needs, friendship groups, and any other information considered important, but not requests for particular teachers based on hearsay about their quality).
>
> **The result**: the new process took a year or 2 to establish, but in the end, it better served the needs of the students and involved a more effective use of parent voice and teacher expertise in class allocation. This change in process also set a change in leadership expectation at the school; in the context of historical parent voice in decision-making. It raised the conversation to one of discussion and decision-making based on evidence and data about how each child can best be served in terms of meeting their individual needs within the broader class and school context.

School leaders spend a great deal of time considering and responding to context to improve the operation and outcomes of a school. This can be done to manage a problem or issue that has arisen or undertaken more strategically to improve on the way things have been managed in the past. As discussed, context can include a variety of levels at or beyond a school; at an individual staff or school community member level, at a group level within or beyond the school, at a whole-school level, or at a level external to the school. What sort of things might be within our span of control to change and how might we adjust leadership to meet an identified need or improvement opportunity? Some examples that come to mind include:

- adjusting a school's leadership structure to account for a change in education policy or strategy; for example, creating a formal leadership position to lead a newly funded initiative
- changing or adding to the school's leadership learning program; for example, to better engage with student voice

- altering or adding to a school leadership decision-making process; for example, including parent involvement or consultation on changes to school curriculum.

As noted earlier in this chapter, the interplay between leadership and context is complex, and as Hallinger notes, 'Optimizing leadership practices for a specific school at a specific moment in time must take into account multiple layers of the widely shared context (i.e. institutional, community, socio-cultural, political, etc.) as well as the personal resources of the leader. Indeed, the task of specifying a "context-specific set of actions" is akin to peeling back layers of an onion.'[25] I do not mean to imply in this book that adjusting and fitting leadership to context will be easy, but I am in total agreement with Roland S Barth when he argues that 'School people carry around extraordinary insights about their practice—about discipline, parental involvement, staff development, child development, leadership, and curriculum. I call these insights "craft knowledge"'.[26] Using this 'craft knowledge' can help us use leadership context to improve school and student outcomes.

The literature on context and leadership

There is a variety of discussion in the literature about 'context and leadership' that is worth considering as you develop a leadership ecosystem:

- *The personal and professional skills and dispositions of staff*: Kristina Brezicha and colleagues argue that 'Effectively leading a complex and dynamic system requires leaders who understand and respect how individuals make sense of their work while working within the context of their social environment and boundaries of the school setting. Therefore, school leaders

---

25 Hallinger (2018) p. 19
26 Barth RS (2006) 'Improving relationships within the schoolhouse', *Educational Leadership. Improving Professional Practice*, 63(6):8–13, http://www.ascd.org/publications/educational-leadership/mar06/vol63/num06/Improving-Relationships-Within-the-Schoolhouse.aspx; Hallinger (2018)

need to be aware of a teacher's professional philosophy, prior experiences, and social network, which will all affect the types of supports that they need.'[27]

- *The personal and professional skills and dispositions of leaders*: Leithwood and colleagues suggest that leaders have a '... person-specific context [which] consists of the job knowledge, skills, attitudes and experience a leader brings to the job. The leader's life experience and personal resources act as a prism through which information, problems, opportunities and situations are filtered and interpreted.'[28]
- *The impact of increasing collective and shared leadership practice*: can lead to improved leader influence, working relationships and professional community, and an associated improvement in student achievement or conditions for improved student achievement.[29] Chapter 1 contains further information about collective school leadership, and Chapter 5 provides guidance about evaluating and monitoring a leadership ecosystem.
- *The importance of considering external context influences*: Pont argues that 'In sum, the role that school leadership plays is key for well-functioning schools but how school leadership is practiced depends on the education system and policy context … As the 21st century advances so does the external context. Governance is increasingly complex, and accountability is shifting towards professional responsibility. Schools engage increasingly with horizontal professional practices among their staff—and work in a more networked approach across schools. This will undoubtedly also change the role of school leaders, who will have to navigate, interpret and make sense of these for their school, and work with their education professionals in new ways.'[30]
- Shelby Cosner and colleagues throw some light on *the potential value of schools engaging with external 'intermediary organisations'*,

---

27 Brezicha K, Bergmark U and Mitra DL (2015:29) 'One size does not fit all: differentiating leadership to support', *Educational Administration Quarterly*, 51(1):96–132, doi.org/10.1177/0013161X14521632
28 Hallinger (2018:7)
29 Seashore et al. (2010)
30 Pont (2020:166)

arguing that 'Through their direct work with schools, especially the most vulnerable schools, these organizations straddle the larger ecosystem and the local schoolhouse, becoming a primary and proximal conduit of external leadership resources into schools.'[31]

- *Selecting the 'right' leaders for a particular school or school context*: given that context can change over time and school leaders may need to take on different leadership roles within a school or in different areas of the school, it would seem that a balance between selecting leaders for 'fit to context' and a 'capacity to adjust' their leadership to suit changed context is important. Alexander and colleagues argue that 'Only after carefully defining the business challenge, including the underlying conditions in which executives will have to lead, is it possible to understand what kind of leader is needed.'[32] The Indeed Editorial Team suggest, 'To lead their team well, managers and supervisors may need to either adapt their leadership style to the current situation or delegate some of their leadership responsibilities to a coworker.'[33]

- *The importance of accurate and timely context data and evidence*: gathering and engaging with the data and best evidence about your leadership context can ensure that leaders are using the full range of information to inform leadership design and practice. Schools are often awash with data, including things like school performance, student outcome, and teacher and student opinion data. The ACER Principal Performance Improvement Tool[34] advocates a reflective process that includes 'triangulation of evidence' for principals to reflect on their leadership. Processes such as these can provide guidance for all leaders to sift through and focus on relevant leadership data and evidence.

---

31 Cosner S, Whalen S, Richard M and Hebert M (2021:11) *Exploring educational ecosystems through the lens of intermediary organisations: insights for policy and practice*, WISE, Qatar Foundation, accessed 23 February 2022. https://www.wise-qatar.org/exploring-educational-ecosystems-through-the-lens-of-intermediary-organizations/
32 Alexander et al. (2017:2)
33 Indeed Editorial Team (2022) *Contingency theory of leadership: definition and models*, Indeed.com, accessed 28 July 2022. https://www.indeed.com/career-advice/career-development/contingency-theory-of-leadership
34 ACER (2018a:2)

- *Quality use of data and evidence*: Monash University (Q Project) suggests that it is not just a matter of having the right data and evidence; it is important that there is quality use of that evidence: 'Quality use of research evidence in education is defined as the thoughtful engagement with and implementation of appropriate research evidence, supported by a blend of individual and organisational enabling components within a complex system.'[35] Giving due consideration to how you are using the evidence and data available in your leadership practice can help improve the operation and impact of your leadership approach.
- *Effectively communicating and consulting with members of a school's context*: involves effectively engaging a school's stakeholders to ensure the 'what', 'how' and 'when' of leadership change is made within the leader's context. Alexander and colleagues suggest that 'An evaluation of the context also should consider stakeholder expectations, including those of employees, investors and customers. Failing to explicitly articulate these expectations as part of the context can lead to problems later on'.[36] Katie Rouse suggests that 'Families, teachers, and communities all have varying perspectives on what the school year can and should hold for students. School leaders need to balance these voices in decision-making through effective and authentic stakeholder engagement.'[37]

Activity 4 has been developed to help you consider how aspects of your individual or collective school leadership context could be used to modify leadership practice to improve school and student outcomes. The information resulting from undertaking this activity can be used in developing 'leadership improvement focuses' discussed in Chapter 7.

---

35 Monash University (2020b:1) Q Project: Quality use of research evidence framework – Summary, Monash University Faculty of Education, Victoria, Australia, accessed 29 July 2022. https://www.monash.edu/education/research/projects/qproject/publications/quality-use-of-research-evidence-framework-qure-report
36 Alexander et al. (2017:4)
37 Rouse K (2020) *A school leader's guide to effective stakeholder engagement*, Bellwether Education Partners, accessed 9 June 2021. https://bellwethereducation.org/publication/school-leader's-guide-effective-stakeholder-engagement

Activity 4: Using leadership context to improve outcomes

Purpose: To consider how to use identified leadership context priorities to improve school and student outcomes.

ACTIVITY

Step 1: For each of the priorities identified in 'Activity 3: Identifying school leadership context priorities', establish an approach to leadership context improvement, noting:

- *the nature of the change*: What exactly needs to change and is it within your power to make that change?
- *the extent of the change*: How much needs to change?
- *the timing of the change*: When and for how long?

Record your agreed responses to these questions. Note: add and/or delete priorities as necessary depending on whether or not they will improve school and/or student outcomes.

Step 2: Consider the leadership context literature (noted in 'The literature on context and leadership' above) for each of the priorities developed in Step 1: staff and leader dispositions, the value of improved collective school leadership, external school influences, leader selection, data quality and use, and effective consultation and communication.

4. Create the foundations of a leadership ecosystem

Understanding and designing a leadership approach that considers the particular characteristics of a school's unique circumstances will ensure that leadership in a school is fit for purpose; aligned with the school and broader community's economic, social, cultural and political circumstances, needs and aspirations. It can create a leadership system that is dynamic and responsive to its various contexts and changes within that context and can position leadership so that it is better placed to deliver improved school and student outcomes. Leithwood and colleagues propose that 'A school leader's main question should always be "Under these conditions, what should I do?"'[38]

The effectiveness of any leadership approach will in part be influenced by the context in which that leadership operates, and the fidelity of development and implementation of the approach. What works in one school may not necessarily work in another or may require modification to be successful. Activity 5 provides an opportunity to begin documenting an ecosystem leadership approach. Subsequent chapters will build on the work done in this activity to create a leadership ecosystem overview.

Activity 5: An ecosystem leadership approach to the school context

Purpose: To create a foundation on which to establish an ecosystem approach to school leadership.

ACTIVITY

Combine the information from Activities 1 to 4 to create an overview document of your leadership context (individual and/or collective). It should include the following sections:

1. Context overview (use information from Activities 1 and/or 2).
2. Content priorities (use information from Activities 3 and 4).

---

[38] Leithwood et al. (2019:6)

If we are to truly effect improvement in leadership impact and performance, then we need to personalise and target that improvement for every school; to work with and within each school's unique context and for schools to work beyond their gates with other schools and with school systems and policymakers. We improve an education system by ensuring that we lift the performance of each school. The Organisation for Economic Co-operation and Development's (OECD) Implementation Framework for Effective Change in Schools contends, 'that education policy has become more complex and requires balancing traditional top-down implementation processes with more bottom-up approaches that leave room for co-construction and local adaptation.'[39]

Context plays a significant part in how leadership is designed and enacted. By developing a leadership approach that is firmly rooted in the context of that leadership; an approach that responds to its context and changes in that context, and which in turn positively impacts on that context; we can create leadership that is fit for purpose and can directly impact on things that matter for improving school and student outcomes.

In Chapters 1 and 2, we identified leadership context as one of the 5 ecosystem leadership elements that can be used to assist us to develop a more systematic approach to leadership in a school, as summarised here.

> *Leadership context*: understanding internal and external school circumstances to create the foundations of a leadership approach that is aligned with the needs, interests and aspirations of a school community.
> - A school's leadership ecosystem should identify and analyse the internal and external contexts in which the leadership ecosystem operates to ensure that the school's leadership design and practice is aligned with the circumstances of that school and its broader community, ensuring that it is 'fit for purpose'.
>
> Continued ▶

---

39 OECD (Organisation for Economic Co-operation and Development) (2020a:1) 'An implementation framework for effective change in schools', *OECD Education Policy Perspectives*, no. 9, OECD Publishing, Paris, https://doi.org/10.1787/4fd4113f-en

- Leadership contexts include demographic, sociocultural, historical and performance information, together with the identified needs, interest and aspirations of that community, and the broader education, economic, environmental and social systems in which the school operates.
- Leadership context should consider how the school's leadership approach is impacted by local and broader contexts and how the leadership approach impacts on those contexts.
- Leadership context development will benefit from the development of an explicit stakeholder management plan. It is important to identify who has an interest in and an impact on a school and its leadership, and anyone or any organisation that will be impacted by what the school does and how leadership operates. Identifying and planning for how leadership will interact with the key stakeholders that are a part of a school's context will ensure that leadership relationships within, across and beyond the school are successfully harnessed and managed.

In Chapter 5 we take what we have learnt about leadership context and use it to assist us to develop a leadership vision and a set of 'leadership principles' for a school.

CHAPTER 5
Leadership vision

> *Leadership vision* — the overarching purpose and foundational principles of the ecosystem design and operation.

Creating a shared vision of, and principles for, leadership at a school; creating clarity for both leaders and followers about what leadership stands for and how it should operate at the school.

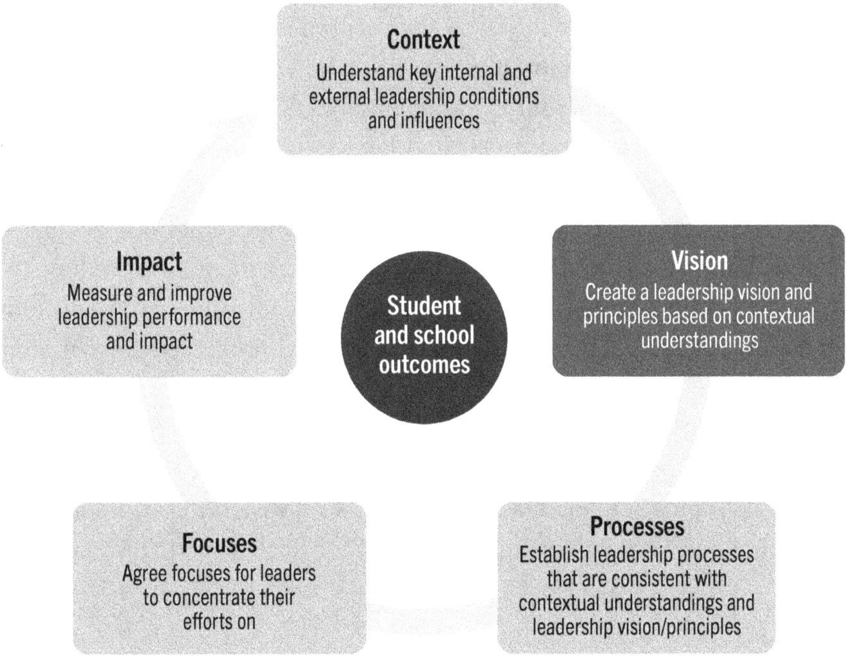

Context
Understand key internal and external leadership conditions and influences

Vision
Create a leadership vision and principles based on contextual understandings

Processes
Establish leadership processes that are consistent with contextual understandings and leadership vision/principles

Focuses
Agree focuses for leaders to concentrate their efforts on

Impact
Measure and improve leadership performance and impact

Student and school outcomes

Figure 5.1 Leadership vision

I found my calling at teacher's college; I loved it, and I had a voracious appetite to learn, develop and make an impact. 'Who I was' underpinned my developing moral purpose. This purpose served to drive my work and led me to where I was going, keeping my integrity and sense of self intact. I recall those early days as a principal, when hard decisions had to be made, wondering what might enable me to 'walk tall' at the end of the day. The answer to this was the manner in which I was leading, and that the direction of that leadership was consistent with my principles.

Can one exist without knowing what you represent, what your 'non-negotiables' look like? What bad or great look like to you, or by compromising your leadership principles (explicitly or implicitly)? I think one probably can, but in my experience, people are less likely to follow you, as your leadership will be confused and tend to wobble and break when things get tough. I have seen some charismatic and hardworking leaders who knew what they wanted, who espoused a clear set of leadership values and principles, but in the crucial moments, their veneer lacked the capacity to remain true to their leadership principles.

The value of an explicit 'vision' for a school is, according to Carmen Mombourquet, well documented in education literature. His findings from a study of 27 elementary, middle school and high school principals from Alberta, Canada '… lends support to findings concerning effective leadership for learning practices and where vision for school has been noted as an essential skill of new and experienced school leaders.'[1] Shelley Kirkpatrick asks, 'Why is the vision statement so prevalent in theories, models, and practical advice? They all identify the vision statement as a crucial factor for enhancing organisational performance.'[2]

A clearly articulated vision for leadership in a school can improve the quality and impact of that leadership. Adding in an explicit set of 'principles' that guide the practical expression of the leadership vision creates a foundation for leadership that is consistent, comprehensive and coherent. This leadership vision and associated principles outline

---

1 Mombourquette C (2017:19) 'The role of vision in effective school leadership', International Studies in Educational Administration, *Journal of the Commonwealth Council for Educational Administration & Management*, 45(1)
2 Kirkpatrick S (2016:21) *Build a better vision statement: extending research with practical advice*, Lexington Books

what leadership in the school stands for and aspires to, and detail the leadership development and practice within, across and beyond the school. They provide an overarching view about the purpose of leadership at the school and the way leadership will be practiced. Documenting and communicating the school's leadership vision and principles can provide leadership clarity for the school and broader community, an opportunity for school leaders to be held to account for their practice, and a basis from which to improve the quality and impact of leadership.

Natural ecosystems have been successful for millions of years because of the manner in which each ecosystem operates. While there are operational principles that are common among ecosystems, a desert is different from a rainforest or a grassland. Each ecosystem has grown and developed such that each has been able to thrive and flourish in the place in which that ecosystem exists. While there is no explicit 'vision' for each ecosystem, it is possible to identify each by their individual nature and ascertain how they develop for the benefit of the species that exist within that ecosystem.

Being clear about 'what', 'why' and 'how' you operate has significant benefits.

In this chapter we explore 4 key areas for developing a leadership vision and associated principles for both your individual leadership and for the collective leadership of a group or school. We will work through the following steps:

1. Understand your leadership style.
2. Develop your leadership vision.
3. Develop your leadership principles.
4. Build your leadership ecosystem.

1. Understand your leadership style

As proposed in the Introduction, 'leadership style' is as individual as our fingerprints and changes as we change. We all bring to our leadership a range of skills, motivations, knowledge and dispositions. Understanding who we are and what drives us is not an easy undertaking. Developing a comprehensive and accurate view of ourselves, and how that impacts our leadership will never be a prefect science but spending time reflecting on what drives us and what is important to us is worth the investment.

Throughout my career I have been fortunate to participate in a range of formal personality tests and work preference instruments; things like the Myers-Briggs Type Indicator,[3] Four Rooms of Change,[4] Hogan Development Survey (HDS),[5] DiSC personal assessment tool,[6] as well as emotional intelligence and problem-solving assessments. As advised in most of these assessments, the results are not necessarily definitive or prescriptive, but they do provide preferences or indicators for how we prefer or are likely to operate under certain conditions. They can provide us with insights into how we are likely to lead in various contexts and how we can enhance or moderate certain behaviours or dispositions. One of the more insightful learnings for me in recent years was identified in the HDS where a behavioural tendency for 'mischief when bored, under stress or fatigued' was identified. I remember it being such a revelation; something I had never consciously identified but is obvious now I think about it. The HDS provided me with ideas about how to use this disposition for benefit and to moderate this tendency to manage negative outcomes. Using formal personality and preference instruments is one way to get to know your behavioural and leadership preferences and dispositions and can help inform how you operate as an individual leader. When the results of these instruments are shared and analysed within a leadership collective, they can be used to plan a collective approach to leading.

There are also informal sources of information and ways to help establish your beliefs, what is important to you, and how you would prefer to operate as a leader or part of a group of leaders. These include understanding the values that drive you and your ethical

---

3   The Myers-Briggs Company (n.d.) *All about the Myers-Briggs (MBTI) assessment*, accessed 28 July 2022. https://ap.themyersbriggs.com/themyersbriggs-all-about-the-mbti-assessment.aspx
4   Four Rooms of Change (n.d.) *This is The Four Rooms of Change – the real deal that helps you manage change*, accessed 27 July 2022. https://fourroomsofchange.com/
5   Hogan Assessments (n.d.) *Hogan development survey*, accessed 28 July 2022. https://www.hoganassessments.com/assessment/hogan-development-survey/
6   disc profile (n.d.) *What is DiSC: deepen your understanding of yourself and others*, accessed 27 July 2022. https://www.discprofile.com/what-is-disc/

understandings (i.e. your principles and beliefs),[7] identifying your context in understanding the literature and research on improving outcomes and working out how that might apply in your school, and engaging in effective student, teacher and community voice to understand what others think is most critical for the school.[8] It might also include some reflections about the things you enjoy and things that challenge you when leading. For instance, I know that I love ambiguity; I love it when things are messy, and I have a particular dislike for role clarity as I believe it can limit leadership. I know that this annoys some people. Together, this sort of information, analysis and reflection can help you decide what the 'critical elements' of your leadership should be, how your leadership approach can operate most effectively; to understand what is important and what is not. Tom Fox writes that 'A friend of mine sometimes uses sailing as a metaphor for leadership. He is fond of saying that exceptional leaders will identify a true north – their essential leadership principles – to navigate calm or rough waters.'[9]

Activity 6 on p. 82 can assist you to identify the things that are important to you about your leadership. Just a reminder that, as suggested in Chapter 4, the activities in this book are designed to be modified to suit individual context or need, or you could create your own activity. Importantly, working through these activities allows you develop the key elements of a leadership ecosystem.

---

7   The Ethics Centre (2020) *What is ethics?*, accessed 28 July 2022. https://www.youtube.com/watch?v=u399XmkjeXo
8   See 'servant leadership discussion' p. 109, Munby S (2017) *Principled leadership in challenging times*, Victorian Academy of Teaching and Leadership, accessed 28 July 2022. https://www.academy.vic.gov.au/learning-resources/principled-leadership-challenging-times
9   Fox T (7 February 2013) 'Developing leadership principles', The Washington Post, accessed 14 July 2021. https://www.washingtonpost.com/national/on-leadership/developing-leadership-principles/2013/02/07/3ddf61e2-7171-11e2-ac36-3d8d9dcaa2e2_story.html

Activity 6: Identifying your leadership position

Purpose: To assist you to better understand your individual and/or collective school leadership position.

ACTIVITY

Individual

Step 1: Write down all the things that are important to you in the way you lead, and then all the things that are not important to you. This is a brainstorming activity, so go wild!

Step 2: Gather information from leadership instruments that you may have been involved in and make a consolidated list of leadership preferences that arise from those instruments. If you have not undertaken any leadership assessments such as these, then you could ask some trusted colleagues to list things that they think are important and not important to you in the way you lead and/or any preferences they have seen in terms of the way you lead. Note: even if you have some leadership instrument information, you may still like to undertake this colleague task.

Step 3: Using the information gathered in Steps 1 and 2 and any other information you think relevant (readings, conversations with others, recent experiences), craft a statement about the key elements of your leadership 'true north' – try to keep this to 2 or 3 paragraphs.

Step 4: Test your statement with one or more trusted colleagues and get their feedback. Modify the statement depending upon the feedback you get.

Collective

Step 1: Each of the individuals in the collective complete the 'individual' Steps 1 to 4 above.

Step 2: Share the leadership 'true north' statements, you may like to use the Ladder of Inference* protocol to guide the discussion and create a collective statement, noting that this may require some significant compromise, but should represent the critical elements of the group's shared leadership position.

---

* Mulder P (2018) *Ladder of Inference*, ToolsHero, accessed 2 June 2021. https://www.toolshero.com/decision-making/ladder-of-inference/

2. Develop your leadership vision

Being clear about what you want your leadership to achieve, and being able to communicate that, provides stakeholders with an explicit statement of what you want your leadership to look like and how you will achieve it.

Schools, like many other organisations, are generally not strangers to vision and mission statements. As Kelly-Ann Allen and Peggy Kern write, 'Vision and mission statements … make a public statement about what the school sees as the purpose of education and how students should learn. Vision statements outline a school's objectives, and mission statements indicate how the school aims to achieve that vision.'[10] A vision statement can include a variety of individual and organisational elements, including purpose, goals, key objectives and approaches, values, principles, a representation of what an organisation stands for, and/or a future desired position.[11]

While it is likely that your school will have a vision and/or mission statement, it is argued here that establishing a specific and separate 'leadership vision', and where appropriate, a collective school leadership vision, will provide you with an opportunity to reflect on and come to conclusions about your leadership approach. It can assist you to create an overarching view about your leadership; to be clear about the purpose of your leadership and how it should be enacted. It can assist to identify the broad parameters for making decisions, working with others, leading school initiatives and improvements (particularly as they relate to your school's strategic plan), and for improving school and student outcomes (see Chapters 8 and 9). Publishing your individual and collective school leadership context provides an opportunity for school leaders to be held to account for their leadership practice, and provide guidance for leaders new to the school, stepping into temporary leadership positions and for informal leadership practice across the school. The Indeed Career Guide argues that 'A leadership vision is important for two reasons:

---

10 Allen K and Kern P (15 June 2018) 'School vision and mission statements should not be dismissed as empty words', *The Conversation*, accessed 11 June 2021. https://theconversation.com/school-vision-and-mission-statements-should-not-be-dismissed-as-empty-words-97375

11 Allan and Kern (2018); OECD (2020a); Bain & Company (2018) *Management tools: mission and vision statements*, Bain and Company Insights, accessed 17 June 2021. https://www.bain.com/insights/management-tools-mission-and-vision-statements/; Mombourquette (2017)

It provides inspiration and motivation to keep going. People are likely to work harder when they have targets to meet. Leadership vision sets goals for the team to accomplish within a given period.

It offers clarity and focus. It is easy to convince people to work when showing the direction or a defined destination. There are so many life distractions that divert our attention from what we want to achieve. With a powerful leadership vision, a leader is able to act on their vision to accomplish their set goals. A compelling vision can also help keep team members engaged.'[12]

As described in Chapter 4, I decided to become a teacher because of a range of things that I was passionate about; things that were underpinned by personal and professional values and beliefs. These matters clearly framed the manner of my teaching and leadership. It was not until later in my career, however, that I spent time identifying and analysing exactly what these values and beliefs were and how they influenced and impacted on my leadership. Only when I began to work with my leadership coach, Richard, did I really start to explicitly consider the nature of my leadership and to explore its foundations, the manner of its enactment and its potential impact on people, teams and organisations and the stakeholders I interacted with.

Richard worked with me on several levels to help me understand the various things that influenced my leadership, and we considered the relationship between vision, values, behaviours, culture and outcomes. Being explicit and overt about what I wanted from myself, the way I wanted to act and be known, and what I expected of others, was incredibly helpful for improving my leadership. In retrospect, I think I could have dived deeper into this work and not only identified more clearly what I wanted my leadership to look and act like, but also could have clearly communicated my individual leadership vision and principles, understood the nature of my colleagues' leadership, and

---

12 Indeed Career Guide (2021) *What are leadership vision statements?*, Indeed.com, accessed 22 June 2021. https://www.indeed.com/career-advice/career-development/leadership-vision-statements

together with some of my leadership teams, developed a collective vision and set of principles.

Developing a leadership vision should include being aware of the context you are leading in, including the vision of the school and the school's network, district, system or government visions, and consulting with and working collaboratively with key stakeholders.[13] The Indeed Career Guide argues that for a vision to be viable and inspire people, it must meet a few fundamental criteria. It must be unique, simple, direct, inspiring, future-oriented, positive, inclusive and actionable.[14]

Advice about developing a vision statement will often include the idea of developing a separate mission statement, and sometimes the 2 concepts are '… combined to provide a statement of the company's purposes, goals and values. However, sometimes the two terms are used interchangeably'.[15] I have not discussed the idea of creating a mission statement here as I want to keep vision as a high-level aspirational statement. You could also create a leadership mission statement if it suited your need to do so.

Activity 7 will assist you to develop a leadership vision for your context.

Activity 7: Developing a leadership vision

Purpose: To assist you to develop an individual and/or collective school leadership vision.

ACTIVITY

Individual

Step 1: Using the 'true north' statement developed in 'Activity 6: Identifying your leadership position' for reference, create a high-level leadership vision statement. The statement should be aspirational in nature and include your:

- purpose
- key goals

Continued ▶

---

13 OECD (2020a)
14 Indeed Career Guide (2021)
15 Bain & Company (2018)

- approaches
- values
- principles
- future position.

Keep the statement to 2 or 3 paragraphs at most and check that it is unique, simple, directive, inspiring, future-oriented, positive, inclusive and actionable.

Step 2: Test your statement with some trusted colleagues and adjust, depending upon the feedback you get.

Collective

Step 1: Each of the individuals in the collective complete the 'individual' Steps 1 and 2 above.

Step 2: Share the individual leadership vision statements with your group; you may like to use the Ladder of Inference* protocol to guide the discussion; and create a collective statement, noting that this may require some significant compromise, but should represent the critical elements of the group's shared leadership position.

Step 3: Test the vision with some trusted colleagues, both inside and outside the school, and refine using the feedback gathered.

Step 4: Test the vision with key internal and external stakeholders and adjust according to the feedback received.

3. Develop your leadership principles

Developing a set of 'leadership principles' allows you to be explicit about how you expect your leadership to operate. It provides you with a guide for leading, ensuring consistency and coherence of practice and a focus on the things that matter. It can provide the people you lead a clear understanding of how you intend to operate, and it allows them to hold you to account.

When I first took up a principal position, I felt overwhelmed. I had little formal leadership training, was inexperienced at leading from a formal position and there was a lack of support from the department.

---

* Mulder P (2018) *Ladder of Inference*, ToolsHero, accessed 2 June 2021. https://www.toolshero.com/decision-making/ladder-of-inference/

I decided to base all my decisions on what I believed was in the best interests of the school and the students. I remember thinking that if I could do that, then I could live with the hard decisions that needed to be made. However, as I have discussed, much of 'how' I wanted to lead and 'what' was important to me about my leadership was not explicitly communicated to those around me. I was never overt about the things that guided my leadership, including my resolve to base my decision-making on what I thought was in the best interests of the school and students. If I were to state this as a leadership principle now, it would read something like: 'My leadership is centred on the needs and interests of the school and its students'. I remember having a discussion with a colleague about the fact that I did not make decisions quickly and that this frustrated people sometimes (in fact, I preferred to hear a variety of views before deciding). Perhaps if I had clearly communicated this to my colleagues, it may have assisted them to understand that I was not avoiding making decisions, but rather making sure that we had all the information we needed to make the best decision possible. Expressed as a 'leadership principle' this might have looked something like: 'My leadership will balance the timeliness of decision making with gathering sufficient information and data to properly inform a leadership decision'.

If I had been clearer about my vision, my colleagues and the school community would have understood more about what I was doing, how I was operating, and would have been able to hold me to account when my leadership practice was inconsistent. It might have created a conversation about whether the nature of my leadership was effective and how it might be improved; it might have assisted others in developing and improving their own leadership practice; and it might have led to conversations to develop a more collective approach to leadership at the school.

As discussed in Chapter 4, 'context' plays an important part in leadership, and the vision and principles of each organisation should reflect the nature and aspirations of that organisation and its community. Amazon explains that 'Our unique Amazon culture, described by our leadership principles, helps us relentlessly pursue our mission of being

Earth's most customer-centric company ...'[16] Amazon's principles require of its leaders things like learn and be curious, insist on the highest standards, have a backbone; disagree and commit. The Dell Company, alternatively, believes that 'How we lead matters. This is how we lead at Dell ... relationships, drive, judgement, vision, optimism, humility, selflessness.'[17] The principal of Gahanna Lincoln High School in the US cites the following leadership principles for the school: 'Vision, relationships, clear expectations, communication, teamwork and service, accountability and learning.'[18] Each of the principles outlined for each of these organisations has been developed to suit the unique nature, needs and interests of that particular organisation.

If I look back over my 30-plus years of leadership, it is clear that I unwittingly developed a set of principles to guide my leadership, and I suspect that most people do the same over their career. The core principles that developed over my career include:

- *Respect for process*: ensure that there are clear and proper processes, and that leadership adheres to those processes. For example, making sure that staff selection makes proper use of the prescribed selection processes, particularly any merit and equity rules.
- *Ensure care and compassion for all*: being open to and responding sympathetically to the individual needs and circumstance of every person. For example, accommodating and adjusting working conditions based on people's health, family and/or emotional needs.
- *Have a go*: supporting people who want to innovate, create and try new things for themselves, their team, or the organisation more broadly. For example, I was always interested in discussing new ideas or innovations from students, parents, staff or associated organisations. It did not mean that every one of these ideas were

---

16 Amazon (2021) Leadership principles, accessed 29 July 2021. https://www.amazon.jobs/en/principles
17 Dell Technologies (n.d.) *How we work and lead*, accessed 8 July 2021. https://jobs.dell.com/how-we-work-and-lead
18 Carter D (2012) *Leadership principles*, Mr Carter's Office, accessed 5 August 2022. https://dwightcarter.edublogs.org/2012/12/31/leadership-principles/

pursued, but I was always open to a conversation and encouraged people to share.
- *Share leadership*: leadership should not just be for those in positional authority. Encourage and support everyone to lead and to learn about leadership. For example, too often I have seen leaders in formal leadership positions dismiss the valuable contributions that informal leaders could have brought to the table.
- *Use evidence and data*: use relevant and reliable sources of data and evidence in leadership, but do not discount a bit of intuition every now and then (in my opinion, intuition is often the brain using information and making connections in an unconscious manner). For example, through my policy work I became increasingly aware of the importance of data and evidence in leadership, and the capacity for leaders to effectively use that evidence and data.
- *Include and consult*: listening to and including others and creating collaborative leadership in a school can bring enormous value. For example, the OECD provides some excellent advice about inclusive stakeholder engagement,[19] but it does not always need to be as formal as this; just talking to and including others in leading is critical and, as discussed in Chapter 2, collaborative leadership has proven benefits.
- *Leadership should be fun*: it does not mean that it will always be fun, and that everything we do should be fun, but we should be looking for the joy in our work and helping others to find that joy. For example, some of my most memorable leadership experiences have been the joy and laughter shared with my colleagues.

While these principles remained reasonably constant no matter the context I was leading in, I did need to adjust, add or subtract principles to suit different workplaces and circumstances. As a leader of an education policy unit, it was important that my leadership reinforced our principles. There were times when the policy our team were developing

---

19 OECD (2020a)

was being influenced by the opinions of various stakeholders. It was important that my leadership supported and encouraged work that was grounded in evidence and data and that the team held true to that in the briefings, strategies and initiatives being developed. In this leadership role, I needed to adjust my leadership principle regarding 'inclusion and consultation'. The political context of the work was risky, given the profile and power of some of the stakeholders, and I needed to ensure that the team's contact with stakeholders was carefully managed. Alternately, as a principal of a school, I felt much more open to free-ranging discussion and 'brainstorming' of ideas with stakeholders than as a policy manager in a central bureaucracy.

Activity 8 guides the development of leadership principles as an individual leader and/or as a leadership collective.

Activity 8: Developing a set of leadership principles

Purpose: To develop a set of leadership principles.

ACTIVITY

This activity could be undertaken as an individual or a collective.

Step 1: Use the leadership position and vision statements developed earlier in this chapter, together with the True North statement developed in Chapter 4, to identify 5 to 10 leadership principles that could apply to your leadership approach at the school.

Step 2: Test your principles with some trusted colleagues, both inside and outside the school, and refine using the feedback gathered.

Step 3: Test the principles with key internal and external stakeholders and adjust according to the feedback received.

4. Build your leadership ecosystem

As noted in Chapter 4, the activities provided here are an example of work you could undertake; there are many other exercises and processes that you can use to develop a leadership vision and a set of leadership principles. The important thing I am arguing here is that to create an effective 'leadership ecosystem', you need to be clear about your leadership vision, the way you intend your leadership to operate, and how you will communicate that to the people you lead.

Activity 9 takes the context information developed in Chapter 4 and combines it with the vision and principles knowledge you assembled as you worked through this chapter.

> **Activity 9: Building your leadership ecosystem – vision and principles**

Purpose: To further develop your leadership ecosystem overview by adding in your leadership vision and principles to the context work undertaken in Activity 5.

ACTIVITY

Add your leadership vision and principles to the overview document you started in Activity 5.

In Chapters 1 and 2, we identified leadership vision as one of the 5 ecosystem elements that can be used to assist us to develop a more systematic approach to leadership in a school, as summarised here.

> *Leadership vision*: creating a shared vision of, and principles for, leadership at a school; creating clarity for both leaders and followers about what leadership stands for and how it should operate at the school.
> - A leadership vision and associated principles outline what leadership in the school stands for and aspires to, and what guides leadership development and practice within, across and beyond the school. They provide an overarching view about the purpose of leadership at the school and the way leadership will be enacted.
> - A school's leadership vision and principles provide clear statements about how leadership operates within the school,

Continued ▶

> providing clarity for the school and broader community. This affords an opportunity for school leaders to be held to account for their practice, and a basis from which to improve the quality and impact of leadership.
> - A school's leadership vision and principles should be developed in consultation with the school community and key external stakeholders, clearly documented and effectively communicated to the school and broader community.

In Chapter 6 we take what we have learnt about leadership vision and use it to assist us to develop leadership processes for a school.

CHAPTER 6
Leadership processes

> *Leadership processes* — the interconnections and systems within and beyond the ecosystem.

Developing clear, effective and consistent processes that ensure leadership practice at the school is efficient, comprehensive and coherent.

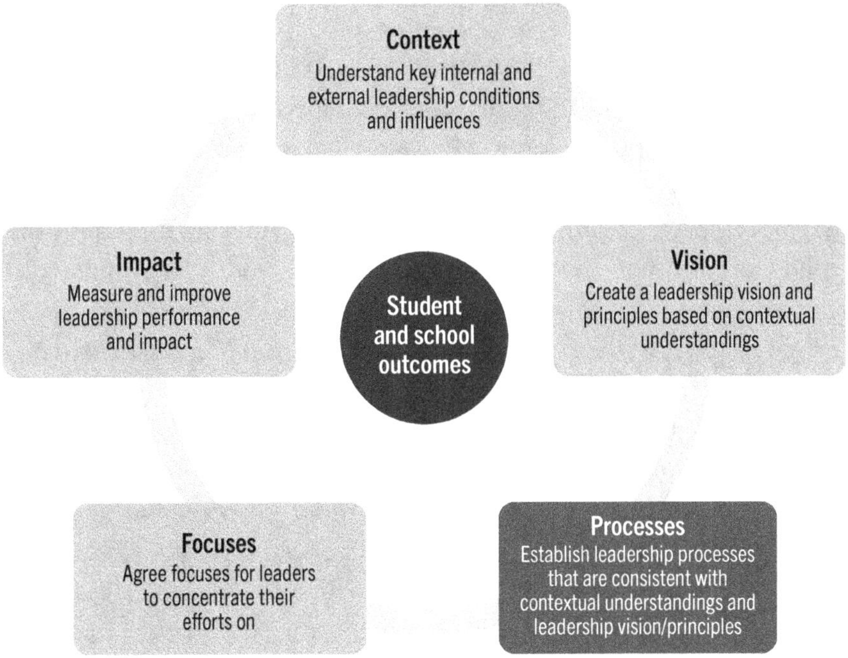

Context
Understand key internal and external leadership conditions and influences

Vision
Create a leadership vision and principles based on contextual understandings

Processes
Establish leadership processes that are consistent with contextual understandings and leadership vision/principles

Focuses
Agree focuses for leaders to concentrate their efforts on

Impact
Measure and improve leadership performance and impact

Student and school outcomes

Figure 6.1 Leadership processes

There are processes and there are processes and then there are processes. There are processes that have been well designed and are easy to operate and those that are not. Processes can enhance how we lead, and they can hinder our leadership; they can contribute to and drive improved school and student outcomes and they can undermine a lot of good work (see Chapters 8 and 9). I am sure we have all experienced the outcomes of good and bad leadership processes.

Ecosystem processes assist systems to operate in integrated and effective ways for the benefit of the members of that ecosystem and for the benefit of the whole system. In a rainforest, for example, we can see complex systems or processes that manage elements of the broader system, including food (food webs and food chains), water cycles (evaporation, condensation, participation), energy cycles (sunlight, photosynthesis, animal and soil respiration, decay); processes that create an integrated and comprehensive management system.

When thinking about processes that operate in schools, it is worth considering how they are designed, how they operate and the outcomes they produce. Some people (including myself, at times) like a bit of chaos and are not inclined to want to be tied to a process, but processes can provide certainly, transparency and clarity about how things will be done, about how decisions will be made, and how we can achieve the things we are seeking to achieve. Chuck Close, speaking about the 'processes' of creating art, suggests that 'If you wait around for the clouds to part and a bolt of lightning to strike you in the brain, you are not going to make an awful lot of work. All the best ideas come out of the process; they come out of the work itself.'[1] In my experience this can be true in education also; schools are great at getting on with the work, creating practical processes to implement improvements in school operation and impact, but I wonder whether we spend enough time on ensuring that our processes are fit for purpose, and that they are as good as we can make them? Do we step back and look more broadly at the set of processes in the school and determine whether they are consistent, integrated, efficient and cover all the matters that they

---

1 in the pursuit of wisdom (20 May 2011) 'Quote by Chuck Close', *in the pursuit of wisdom blog*, accessed 15 July 2021

should? Are we investing sufficient time in making sure our leadership processes across the school are working as well as they could in helping us improve school and student outcomes?

One of the positions I held when I was working in the Victorian Department of Education and Training was as a member of the department's Merit Protection Boards. Our job was to ascertain whether decision-makers had acted in accordance with the various 'rules' when making decisions; had the decision-makers followed the processes properly, and so on. The main work was deciding whether the department's selection procedures had been adhered to for staff selection in schools and the public service. People who had a 'complaint' about the process and how a decision was arrived at could appeal that decision, based on 'evidence' that the 'rules' or 'guidelines' had not been followed properly. It was interesting that on reading the materials presented by the complainant and the decision-maker prior to the hearing, it often seemed like the process had been followed properly. However, once the verbal presentations were made and questions from the panel responded to, it was not always so obvious. Processes can be complex and ensuring that they are effectively developed and implemented can be complicated. Five main things emerged for me from the Merit Protection Boards' experience:

- Even a well-documented process is open to interpretation and can be applied incorrectly.
- The more complex the process, the greater the need for training people to understand and practise the process.
- Never assume that a process has been applied well until you analyse the detail.
- Having a way for people to challenge the process and be heard is important.
- Even though an outcome might appear to be the correct one, if you have not followed the agreed process, it is probably worth doing it again.

These reflections and my experience of leadership and decision-making has led me to consider what a good process looks like. To my mind, a good process includes 6 elements:

1. It is developed in consultation with those who have a vested interest in the process and its outcome/s.
2. It is well designed; timely, accessible, easy to apply, fit for purpose and clear about its intended outcomes.
3. It is clearly documented and communicated.
4. It has capacity to flex to meet varying needs, interests and circumstances.
5. It has capacity to be challenged in reasonable and timely ways.
6. It is monitored, evaluated and adjusted when and if required.

These process elements provide a framework under which leaders can develop and implement leadership processes that are intentionally developed, implemented and improved over time. They can serve to ensure that leadership processes meet the needs and interests of the school and its members; are transparent, fair, efficient and effective; and that they contribute to improved school and student outcomes. It is important to note that there will be other process elements that are important in your context and could be added to or replace the elements identified here. Table 6.1 briefly explores the 6 process elements outlined and the purpose and value of each.

What sort of leadership processes operate in a school, what things might be worth developing as explicit processes, and what things might be identified in a particular context that require the development of specific processes? In my years as a leader in the education sector, there were several common leadership processes that I worked within, developed or modified, across a range of organisations. Some of these processes were developed locally, at a network level or were centrally proscribed. While a number of the processes were decision-making processes, others were processes for development, reflection, evaluation, cooperative and collaborative work. Generally, these processes were in the following areas of school operation:

- *Administration, strategy and governance:* including processes for human resource management, finance, statutory and legislative requirements, policy and infrastructure matters, direction and resources allocation, school governance procedures and leadership structures.

Table 6.1 Process elements

Process element	Purpose and value
1. Developed in consultation with those who have an interest in the process and its outcome/s.	Ensures that the process is based on a broad view about what would work best in particular circumstances, and that the process is 'owned' by key stakeholders.
2. Well designed; timely, easy to apply, accessible, fit for purpose and clear about its intended outcomes.	A well-designed process should be easy to implement and manage and result in outputs that it was designed to achieve. Does the process enhance the school's capacity to improve school and student outcomes?
3. Clearly documented and communicated.	Ensures that people understand the process and know what it is designed to do, how it operates and how they can interact with it.
4. Capacity to flex to meet varying needs, interests and circumstances.	Circumstances and context change, and any process needs to be able to adjust to meet the various changes that impact on the process and/or on which the process impacts.
5. Capacity to be challenged in reasonable and timely ways.	No process is perfect and may at times fail to meet the needs of various stakeholders; an opportunity for people to challenge the design, operation and/or outputs of a process is critical for ensuing voice and equity.
6. Monitored, evaluated and adjusted when and if required.	Ensures the process remains up to date and is improved as necessary to meet changing circumstances and feedback about how well the process works.

- *Improvement*: including processes for professional learning, curriculum development, change management, data and evidence use, and planning and evaluation.
- *Teaching, learning and student wellbeing*: including processes for evidence and data analysis and use, program development/implementation and review, curriculum planning/development and management, student voice, student wellbeing programs, and pedagogical approaches.
- *Community, education sector and government*: including processes to work with the local community, local government services,

education sector organisations, government departments, and education sector associations.

While some of the processes in the organisations I have worked in were well defined, documented and consistently applied, many were ad hoc and undocumented, and varied in their operation, often depending on who was involved in them. What never existed was a consolidated list of the leadership processes operating across the school; what they were, what they were designed for, how they would operate and how they related to each other. Imagine the clarity and coherence for leaders and followers alike of having a defined list of leadership processes; detail about each individual process and the set as a whole. It is not suggested here that every process in a school needs to be defined and documented, but certainly doing so for the more important processes can have significant benefit.

In this chapter we will explore 3 key areas for developing leadership processes to improve our leadership efficacy and further grow the leadership ecosystem at a school. The 3 areas are:

1. Map and analyse leadership processes.
2. Modify and enhance leadership processes.
3. Add leadership processes to your leadership ecosystem.

Undertaking this work should result in a leadership process that operationalises the intentions of your leadership practice and that is consistent with the way you have identified that you want your leadership to operate. These steps could be undertaken as an individual leader or group of leaders managing a team or area in a school and ideally as a leadership collective across a school.

1. Map and analyse leadership processes

Understanding the leadership processes that are currently operating in a school can help us better understand how leadership is being enacted (or not enacted) within, across and beyond the school. This includes looking at how the processes are designed, how they work, where they operate in the school, how well they work and how acceptable the school's stakeholders find them, together with areas of the school where leadership processes are lacking. This can help us improve the way we lead and the impact of our leadership. Karim Shariff and Jenny Davis-Peccoud, in their analysis of decision-making in almost 800 companies, found that '… most companies don't consider themselves very effective at making and executing decisions. Implementation gets bogged down in process. The wrong people are making decisions with the wrong information in the wrong part of the organization. Companies often try to speed things up by shifting boxes and lines on an org chart. But unless they have a clear understanding of where the system is breaking down, those reshuffling efforts rarely bear fruit.'[2] I am certain that in many schools this also holds true, and as is further suggested by Shariff and Davis-Peccoud, 'Improving any of the elements of decision making – quality, speed, implementation – has a direct correlation with financial performance … Getting better at all of those factors has a multiplier effect, meaning that as companies learn how to make and execute high-quality decisions, performance improves rapidly.'[3]

Investing time in understanding a school's leadership processes can assist in working out what needs to change to improve decision-making quality, speed and implementation (among other things) and ultimately the effectiveness of our leadership in improving school performance and school and student outcomes. While decision-making is a critical part of any organisation's leadership processes, it is only one part of a mix of leadership processes. To create a highly functional ecosystem we need to look at individual processes, together with the way in which those individual processes work with each other in an integrated way.

As a principal, there were various instances when I would reflect on the leadership processes in use at the school and consider how they might be amended to improve school and student outcomes. Like so much of my leadership experience, I do not believe that I was particularly holistic or comprehensive in my approach to improving our organisation's leadership approach, including leadership processes.

---

2   Shariff K and Davis-Peccoud J (2012) *Score your organization to improve decision effectiveness*, Bain & Company, accessed 5 July 2022. https://www.bain.com/insights/score-your-organization-ame-info/
3   Shariff and Davis-Peccoud (2012)

I did not really think about the broader set of processes, but tended to focus on improving each individual process, with only minimal thought about consistency in design between each and the manner in which they interacted or impacted on each other. My approach tended to be ad hoc on some occasions and more integrated on others. For example, at one stage we had several staff simultaneously asking to undertake professional learning outside the school. We realised we needed a process for application, allocation and making use of the person's learning when they returned. Our existing process was primarily based on staff identifying things they were interested in and was a bit of a 'first in, best dressed' process. So, we developed a process that considered a range of other school processes and their outcomes or products, including the process for implementing our strategic plan priorities, the program budgeting process, the whole-school professional learning program and our processes for staff performance and development.

The other reflection I have here is that while our school leadership processes were often based on how we could improve school and student outcomes, this was not the central measure we used to design and implement our leadership processes; we did not give direct and explicit consideration to how each process should be designed to improve outcomes.

Given that most systems are dynamic and involve frequent changes, both in internal circumstances and as a response to external influences, the processes we establish need to be able to respond and adjust to those changes and influences.

The development of a leadership ecosystem requires that we integrate the various elements of our leadership approach. Modifying existing leadership processes or creating new ones should be based on the work you have done in developing more explicit views about your leadership context and the vision and principles developed for that context. Examining current leadership processes should involve exploring what they are, what they are designed to do and what might be missing, using criteria such as the leadership context, vision, principles, impact on school and student outcomes, and measures of good process design and implementation. This should assist our understanding of which of our leadership processes are working well and which are not and help us identify what is missing and what needs to change.

Activity 10 provides a suggested approach for examining the leadership processes in use at your school.

It is important to note here that any change to the school's leadership processes should be driven by what suits the school's context, needs and interests; we would not want to make changes just for change's sake, and we should not necessarily respond to influences that are not in the interests of the school, or are in the interests of particular members of the school, unless there were good reasons for that change. For example, schools are constantly introduced to new ideas for improving student learning; we would not want to change a school process to introduce a new approach without first carefully considering what adjustment would be required to ensure efficacy of the approach across the school.

> ### Activity 10: Mapping and analysing the leadership processes currently in use
>
> **Purpose:** To assist you to better understand the leadership processes currently operating at your school and identify areas for improvement.
>
> **ACTIVITY**
>
> **Step 1:** Identify and list the leadership processes in operation at your school. Using these broad areas of school operation might be helpful:
>
> - administration, strategy and governance
> - improvement
> - teaching, learning and student wellbeing
> - community, education sector and government.
>
> **Step 2:** Evaluate each of the processes against the process elements identified in Table 6.1, or your own local set of criteria. Elements include:
>
> - developed in consultation
> - good design features
> - clearly documented and communicated
> - capacity to flex
> - capacity for challenge
> - monitored, evaluated and adjusted.
>
> Continued ▶

Step 3: Now examine each of the processes against the leadership context, vision and principles developed because of your work in Chapters 4 and 5. Are the processes consistent with what you have detailed in this work?

Step 4: List the processes that require modification, replacement or removal, or processes that are not currently in place because of your deliberations in Step 2 and 3.

Step 5: Modify or establish new processes; see 'Activity 11: Modifying and enhancing the leadership processes at your school'.

2. Modify and enhance leadership processes

The way you modify a process can take many forms and is likely to include identifying what needs to change and why, deciding how you would change it, and undertaking that change. There is significant literature about change management,[4] which may or may not be relevant for adjusting or introducing a new leadership process, depending upon the nature and magnitude of the change and the relative importance of the process. Change management models include things like The Eight-step Process for Leading Change,[5] the ADKAR Model,[6] the Bridges Transition Model[7] and Lewin's Change Management Model.[8]

I have not used a particular model of change in the organisations in which I have been a leader, but there are certain elements that are important to me in most of the change I have led, including:

---

4   Cameron E and Green M (2020) *Making sense of change management: a complete guide to the models, tools and techniques of organisational change*, 5th edn, Kogan Page Ltd; Hendricks-Jackson L and Hawkes B (2017) *Nursing professional development review and resource manual*, 4th edn, American Nurses Association; ZenDesk (n.d.) 'Change management models', ZenDesk blog, accessed 28 July 2022. https://www.zendesk.com/blog/change-management-models/
5   Kotter Inc (n.d.) *8-step process for leading change*, Kotter, accessed 28 July 2022. https://www.kotterinc.com/8-steps-process-for-leading-change/
6   Prosci (n.d.) *The Prosci ADKAR model*, Prosci, accessed 28 July 2022. https://www.prosci.com/methodology/adkar
7   Bridges WM (n.d.) *What is transition*, accessed 13 September 2022. https://wmbridges.com/about/what-is-transition/
8   Cummings S, Bridgman T and Brown KG (2015) 'Unfreezing change as three steps: rethinking Kurt Lewin's legacy for change management', *human relations*, 69(1) 33–60, doi:10.1177/0018726715577707

- *Involving key stakeholders throughout the process*: we all know the importance of involving stakeholders in any change process to ensure there is ownership of the change and maximising acceptance of and support for that change. Depending on the nature of the change, stakeholders may include staff, students, parents, the local community, and local or wider education community. The OECD publication, 'An implementation framework for effective change in schools'[9] provides some good advice and a series of helpful guiding questions for effective stakeholder engagement.
- *Spending time understanding the problem or need*: gathering and analysing relevant data helps ensure that we are basing any change on best evidence and that we are clear about the nature or focus of the change. As discussed in Chapters 4 and 5, you may like to consider various methodologies for data management and use.
- *Being strategic in the change implementation process*: this includes the development of a clear process that is explicit about what the potential change might look like and how the change will happen, and clearly communicating that plan to stakeholders. The implementation should be consistent with the context in which you are working. There are a number of ways you could do this. One example is using an online project management tool like Trello[10] to assist with documenting, organising, tracking and communicating the change.
- *Monitoring the new change and adjusting as required*: once the change is completed, it is important to monitor how well the change is operating and whether further changes are required.

Once you have identified your school leadership processes that need to be changed, added or removed, I would recommend that you

---

9   OECD (Organisation for Economic Co-operation and Development) (2020b) *Chapter 1. What TALIS 2018 implies for policy*, vol 2, accessed 18 June 2020. https://doi.org/10.1787/19cf08df-en
10 Trello (n.d.) *Trello helps teams move work forward*, accessed 28 July 2022. https://trello.com/home

consider using the change elements described in the dot points above (and any others you consider relevant) to undertake the identified changes. Importantly, this modification should include consideration of the work you have already done on understanding your leadership context, and the vision and principles you have developed. Activity 11 provides a suggested approach for modifying leadership processes at your school.

As most school leaders are aware, there will inevitably be instances where some people are unhappy with the outcome of a leadership process or decision, but if the process itself is designed and implemented in a manner that is fair, transparent, equitable and in line with the school's leadership vision, principles and focuses and consistent with its context, then at least we are being strategic in the manner in which leadership is enacted in the school. Leadership decisions and actions can also be seen to be made with due process.

Activity 11: Modifying and enhancing the leadership processes at your school

Purpose: To assist you to create a comprehensive set of leadership processes that are consistent, integrated and aligned with your leadership context, vision and principles.

ACTIVITY

Step 1: Establish an agreed process for modifying or developing leadership processes at the school. This could include one of the change models identified in this chapter. Consideration could be given to some of the following suggestions, which are based on the elements of good process described in Table 6.1:

- Ensure stakeholders are aware that a process is being modified or created, and involve them in the following steps, particularly any people or groups who might affected by the process or its results.
- Clarify what problem or need the process is being modified or designed to solve or address.
- Identify who should be involved in the process.
- Identify critical steps in the process, and how they should be undertaken and who should be involved in each step.
- Ensure that the process steps and the overall flow of the process are timely, easy to apply, accessible and fit for purpose.

- Consider the process outputs and how they are to be developed, agreed and communicated.
- Consider whether some form of appeal process is necessary and how it would operate.
- Check the process is consistent with your leadership context, vision and principles.
- Test the process and modify if required.
- Document and communicate details about the revised or new process to the school community.
- Ensure that the process documentation includes an indication of when it is expected that the process will be reviewed again.

Step 2: Modify or establish new processes using the list from Step 4 in 'Activity 10: Mapping and analysing the leadership processes currently in use'.

Step 3: Test your processes with some trusted colleagues, both inside and outside the school, and refine using the feedback gathered.

Step 4: Test the processes with key internal and external stakeholders and adjust according to the feedback received.

3. Add leadership processes to your leadership ecosystem

As noted in Chapter 4, the activities provided here are an example of work you could undertake; there are many other exercises and procedures that you could work through to modify and create new leadership processes.

For Activity 12, take the information you developed as you worked through this chapter and add it to the activities from Chapters 4 and 5 to continue to create a leadership ecosystem for yourself or your school.

Activity 12: Building your leadership ecosystem – processes

Purpose: To further develop your leadership ecosystem by adding your leadership processes information to the context, vision and principles work undertaken in Chapters 4 and 5.

ACTIVITY

Add your leadership processes to the overview document you started in Activity 5.

In Chapters 1 and 2, we identified processes as one of the 5 ecosystem leadership elements that can be used to assist us to develop a more systematic approach to leadership in a school, as summarised here.

> ***Leadership processes***: establishing clear, effective and consistent processes that ensure leadership practice at the school is efficient, comprehensive and coherent.
> - Developing agreed leadership processes ensures that there is efficient, effective and consistent leadership practice and decision-making within, across and beyond the school. It allows us to understand and manage key relationships and interdependencies within and beyond the leadership ecosystem.
> - The processes and systems developed should be applicable to leadership in all areas of the school and, where relevant, should inform and guide leadership processes used beyond the school. Understanding the relationships between various parts of the school's leadership ecosystem is critical in managing important interrelationships more effectively.
> - Leadership processes should be developed in consultation with the school community so that they are aligned with the school's ethos and cultural values, and so they are well understood by all community members.
> - Well-documented, understood and applied leadership processes will provide certainty and coherence for leaders and for the school community. Members of the school community may not always agree with the results of a process, but they will understand that matters have been considered in a consistent and comprehensive manner.

In Chapter 7 we take what we have learnt about leadership processes and use it to assist us to develop leadership focuses for a school.

CHAPTER 7
Leadership focuses

Leadership focuses — the emphases and priorities of the system's operation.

Agreeing on a set of focuses to ensure leadership effort is directed at the things that matter for the school and broader community and are important for improving the school's leadership approach.

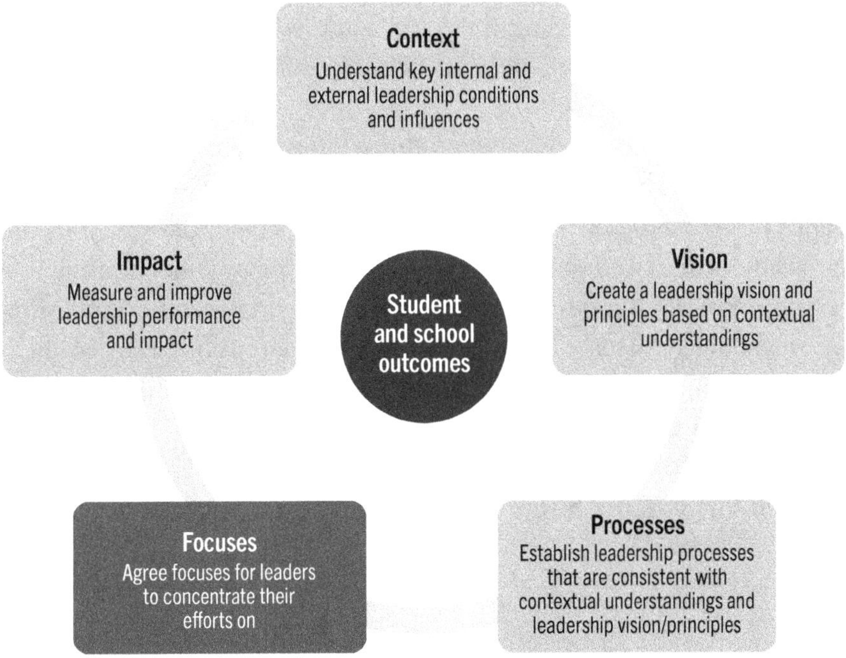

Context
Understand key internal and external leadership conditions and influences

Impact
Measure and improve leadership performance and impact

Student and school outcomes

Vision
Create a leadership vision and principles based on contextual understandings

Focuses
Agree focuses for leaders to concentrate their efforts on

Processes
Establish leadership processes that are consistent with contextual understandings and leadership vision/principles

Figure 7.1 Leadership focuses

Establishing key 'leadership focuses' assists school leaders to target their endeavours and provides transparency for the school community.

Identifying the key focuses of leadership ensures that the right things get the attention they require. It helps concentrate leadership activity on the key outcomes and improvements that have been identified by the school through its improvement planning processes, and on the critical work of improving the leadership approach. It is about leadership focus on both 'what' we should be leading and on 'how' that leadership should be enacted.

You could easily describe the focuses as 'goals' or 'priorities' if that suits your way of thinking. However, those terms are tied to the more formal strategic planning we are usually involved in at the school and may cause 'priority overload' or confusion. While school leaders should certainly focus their leadership efforts on leading the successful implementation of the school's strategic plan priorities, a leadership team needs to focus on matters that improve the operation of the school's leadership approach; both the activity and performance of individual leaders and of groups or teams of leaders within and across a school. Importantly, using the term 'focus/es' here provides a more active emphasis on what the leadership ecosystem is preferencing in terms of its effort.

In trying to improve what we do in schools, there is a tendency to concentrate on a broad range of things, rather than focus on a critical few. I once heard this described as spreading jam on a piece of toast; you can spread the jam so thin that it becomes tasteless, but by concentrating the jam in one area, the taste is magnified. Identifying specific leadership focuses allows us to sustain and deepen our leadership effort on identified matters of importance, rather than spread effort across a broad range of matters that are as a result unlikely to receive the attention they require. In an article about strategic planning priorities, Mark Weber argues that we need to, 'Stop the bloat of strategic initiatives, [and] focus only on top-level priorities'.[1]

---

1   Weber M (2021:3) The 5 most vital strategic planning priorities for renewed focus and growth in 2022, CUInsight, accessed 27 July 2022. https://www.cuinsight.com/the-5-most-vital-strategic-planning-priorities-for-renewed-focus-growth-in-2022.html

Focusing effort is not always a school-driven problem. I am sure many of us have experienced the 'bloat' of system initiatives and programs; as Michael Fullan and Joanne Quinn suggest, 'The problem is not the absence of goals in districts and schools today but the presence of too many that are ad hoc, unconnected, and ever-changing. Multiple mandates from states and districts combine with the allure of grants and innovations, resulting in overload and fragmentation'.[2] It is only in recent years that I have been involved in and led work on explicitly identifying and improving an organisation's leadership focuses. This has involved the collection and analysis of a range of leadership data and the development of actions to improve the work of the leadership team; things like improved communication processes within and beyond the team, improving individual role and team clarity, and being more explicit about when a decision is made by the team.

Increasingly in my time as a school leader in Australia, the strategic planning advice from the Department of Education acknowledged the important of concentrating effort on a smaller number of strategic priorities for school improvement. I must say that while I could see the sense in this approach, I found it hard to do. As educators, I think it is our natural disposition to help everyone, to do everything we can for our students. I remember in the early 1990s when strategic planning was introduced for Victorian Government schools. Subsequent to the analysis of our school data, we identified a range of improvement goals and of course ended up with large list of things that required focus. This list was further increased by several other initiatives that the school was already undertaking. We set about attempting to fit these things into our strategic plan. It was new to us and while we identified some important items, I do not think we were successful in focusing the list on the most important things. We did things like 'grouping' items that required similar action into one big group. But we were not good at dropping off those things that we had already invested effort in and yet probably were not things that were high on our improvement list. Did

---

2   Fullan M and Quinn J (2016:19) *Coherence: the right drivers in action for schools, districts and systems*, Ontario Principals Council and Corwin, CA.

we spread the jam too thin? I think that we most definitely did. Two points are important here:

- It is possible to create what looks like a small set of high-level focuses, but it can be so packed full of things that it is almost impossible to successfully work on everything in that focus area.
- It can be hard to divest yourself of things that are already in place; to stop working on improvement initiatives that are not as important as others.

In this chapter we will explore 4 key areas for developing leadership focuses to improve our leadership efficacy and further develop the leadership ecosystem at a school. The 4 areas are:

1. Understand the value of identifying leadership focuses.
2. Identify leadership focuses.
3. Manage leadership focus effort.
4. Add leadership focus to your leadership ecosystem.

Undertaking this work should result in the identification and implementation of leadership focuses that ensure you are directing leadership effort at achieving both the key elements of your school's strategic plan and the things that matter in terms of improving and sustaining excellence in your leadership practice. The activities and actions outlined in this chapter could be undertaken as an individual leader, a group of leaders managing a team or area, or ideally as a leadership collective across a school.

1. Understand the value of identifying leadership focuses

Being explicitly focused on a limited number of things can have risks and negative impacts. If we do not focus our effort in the right way, monitor our focus effort, and ensure that we are managing any potential downside risks then we may not be as effective and efficient as we desire. Maintaining an oversight of the progress of your focuses, together with being open to other urgent or critical matters, is important for ensuring the sensible and effective management and improvement of school and student outcomes (see Chapters 8 and 9).

That said, identifying and focusing on a set of identified strategic leadership improvements and/or strategic school improvement matters can have significant benefits. It can:

- *Create coherence, clarity and confidence*: rather than scattered leadership activity, a school community can easily identify and understand where and how leadership improvement effort is being directed and how that effort fits with other activity in the school. It can assist school members to understand where to direct their effort, and support and assist the school community to feel confidence in leadership at the school. As Bernard Marr suggests, 'When the strategic goals are laid out in a plan-on-a-page, people remember the goals more easily – they remember the image, they remember the different strategic layers, and they remember the goals that make up each layer'.[3]
- *Deliver improvement effort efficiencies*: by prioritising leadership effort on a smaller number of activities and giving license to school leaders to reduce or cease effort on other areas or activities until the current focuses reach an agreed level of success, or an explicit decision is made to change focus/es.
- *Increase the impact of leadership activity*: by allowing school leaders to maintain a relentless focus on delivery of the agreed tasks and dedicate explicit time and effort to ensuring the success of the leadership activity.
- *Reduce or avoid staff overload*: through permission to concentrate effort on a smaller identified set of areas, staff are not overloaded with a broad range of delivery expectations.
- *Direct resourcing to agreed areas of effort*: to ensure that there are adequate human and financial resources to successfully undertake the improvements identified.

---

3 Marr B (n.d.) *How many strategic goals should a company have?*, Bernard Marr & Co, accessed 8 February 2022. https://bernardmarr.com/how-many-strategic-goals-should-a-company-have/

- *Increase school community commitment:* ensuring that there is broad support for the leadership improvement effort being undertaken at the school.

2. Identify leadership focuses

Identifying leadership focuses involves a broad range of considerations that will be contingent upon the circumstances and context of the school. As has been discussed already in this chapter, the agreed focuses might be a combination of things that can improve collective and individual approaches to leadership, together with focuses based on the improvement strategies and priorities of the school. This might include for example, a focus on improving the school's leadership decision-making processes (a leadership approach improvement) and a focus on improving leadership in embedding a new instructional model (as identified in the school's strategic plan).

Other factors that might assist in identifying key leadership focuses include:

- *Determining* the critical priorities. Derek Lidlow defines a 'critical priority [as] an objective that must be successfully accomplished within a specified amount of time, no matter what.'[4] I would add to that, priorities that are likely to have a significant impact on the functioning of the school, especially as they relate to improved school and student outcomes. It is important to remember here that we are talking about prioritising for major or important strategic developments. There will always be critical day-to-day matters that must be attended to as a priority for leaders, such as health, safety and wellbeing matters, and emergency situations.
- Ensuring that the leadership focuses fit with other school priorities, including the school's strategic plan, and avoiding or managing any potential conflict or clashes that may arise in the effort required to achieve the school's various priorities and focuses.

---

4 Lidow D (13 February 2017) 'A better way to set strategic priorities', *Harvard Business Review*, accessed 10 February 2022. https://hbr.org/2017/02/a-better-way-to-set-strategic-priorities

- *Considering* whether the leadership effort can be and/or needs to be addressed in the short, medium or longer term. Allocating the list of identified focuses into various 'time horizons' may assist in working out what and when to focus your leadership effort on. Nicholas Kachaner and colleagues suggest that 'It is important to think about strategy at different time horizons. Each has different goals and requires different approaches, a different frequency, and the involvement of different people. Much of the frustration expressed about strategic-planning processes arises when companies try to address the long, medium, and short terms through a single, inflexible process.'[5]
- *Developing* the list of leadership focuses collaboratively with the school community, ensuring involvement in the development, and the consequent ownership of the 'what', 'why' and 'how' of the agreed leadership focuses.

Identifying leadership focuses should reflect an understanding of your leadership context, be consistent with your leadership vision and principles, and align with the leadership processes that operate within and across your school. If you have worked through the activities in Chapters 4 to 6 (or designed your own), then you could start with that information to begin identifying what leadership should be focused on in Activity 13.

Activity 13: Identifying leadership focuses

Purpose: To assist you to identify a set of leadership focuses.

ACTIVITY

Work with selected stakeholders to:

Step 1: Brainstorm a list of potential leadership focuses using:

Continued ▶

---

5   Kachaner N, King K and Stewart S (2016) *Four best practices for strategic planning*, Boston Consulting Group, accessed 26 July 2022. https://www.bcg.com/en-au/publications/2016/growth-four-best-practices-strategic-planning

- Information from the activities in Chapters 4 and 6. What was important in your leadership context? What was important to you in terms of your leadership vision and principles, both individually and collectively?
- Available data on leadership performance.
- Leadership requirements necessary to successfully deliver the school's strategic plan and any other improvement initiatives operating or planned.

Step 2: Consider the list developed in Step 1 and retain those that are critical priorities (see description of a critical priority in the bulleted points above), and those that are likely to have the greatest potential to improve school and student outcomes.

Step 3: Identify time horizons for each of the priorities, and document why these focuses have been chosen and how they will be enacted in practice.

Step 4: Check the list against your school strategic plan and other improvement initiatives across the school to ensure alignment and to avoid potential clashes.

Step 5: Test the final list of focuses with key stakeholders, and adjust the focuses based on any feedback received.

3. Manage leadership focus effort

Is there anything more annoying than putting significant effort and energy into something, only to see it wasted when a new direction, initiative or idea arrives on the scene? It has been a frustration of mine and of many of my colleagues over the years when an education authority or a new government decides to refocus effort in a different direction. At times, I believed that we were close to implementing significant improvements across the school system, only to have the program or initiative abandoned and be required to do something new. There is a fine balance between knowing when to adjust or change a focus and when to 'push on'. While school leaders will not always have control over what initiatives, programs or policies are mandated, it is important they are able to sustain, adjust or change focus when it is within their power to do so, and there is clear evidence about the need to sustain or otherwise.

Managing leadership focuses requires considered and explicit attention. It is important to understand whether the focus is having impact, whether it continues to be the most critical thing to focus on, and to decide when to maintain, adjust or change focus. Decision-making here is likely to involve a broad range of considerations; it is unlikely to be a perfect science, but there are several things that may prove useful in helping to manage the focuses of your leadership activity and effort:

- *Communicate*: keep the focuses uppermost in leaders' minds so they maintain their effort and attention on the agreed focuses. Ensure that the school community is kept informed of the progress of the various priorities and consulted on changes of focus.
- *Celebrate*: we all love positive reinforcement.
- *Monitor*: data and evidence about the success and the leadership effort is critical. This provides information to inform decision-making on adjusting or changing focuses. (Chapter 8 discusses processes and strategies for measuring progress and the impact of leadership.)
- *Persevere*: sometimes the hardest thing to do is get to the end. Maintain the rage, avoid changing unless necessary and maintain a relentless focus.
- *Consider*: is adjustment required, rather than just dropping and starting anew?
- *Plan*: for changing focuses to ensure adequate time for consultation, effective implementation and change management and resourcing. Only consider removing something if really necessary.
- *Prepare*: for leadership focus transition as a focus is nearing achievement. Do not leave it too late.

4. Add leadership focuses to your leadership ecosystem

As noted in Chapter 4, the activities provided here are an example of work you could undertake. There are many other exercises and processes that you could work through to modify and identify and sustain your leadership focuses.

Take the information you developed as you worked through this chapter and add it to the information from Chapters 4 to 6 in Activity 14 on p. 116 to continue to create a leadership ecosystem for yourself or your school.

> **Activity 14: Building your leadership ecosystem – focuses**
>
> **Purpose:** To further develop your leadership ecosystem by adding your leadership focuses information to the context, vision and principles work undertaken in Chapters 4 to 6.
>
> **ACTIVITY**
>
> Add your leadership focuses to the overview document you started in Activity 5.

In Chapters 1 and 2, we identified leadership focuses as one of the 5 ecosystem leadership elements that can be used to assist us to develop a more systematic approach to leadership in a school, as summarised here.

> *Leadership focuses*: agreeing on a set of focuses to ensure leadership effort is directed at the things that matter for the school and broader community and are important for improving the school's leadership approach.
> - Establishing the key focuses for the school's leadership effort assists leaders to target and improve their endeavours and provides transparency for the school community about what leadership will be focused on.
> - Identifying the key focuses of leadership ensures that the right things get the attention they require and helps concentrate leadership activity on key outcomes and improvements. It is suggested here that 'leadership focuses' should include 2 major areas:
>   - school improvement priorities identified by the school through its improvement planning processes
>   - improvements to the school's leadership approach.
> - It goes without saying that leadership should be investing significant effort on improving school and student outcomes, but if we are to continue to improve how leadership operates at a school then we also need to identify priority leadership focuses.

> To improve leadership practice and impact we need to be explicit about what we are working on improving.
> - In terms of identifying the key areas for leadership focus, it is important that leadership concentrates its efforts on a discrete number of critical areas rather than a broad range of things. There is a tendency in schools to try to do everything. Identifying specific leadership focuses allows us to sustain and deepen our leadership effort on identified matters of importance, rather than spread effort across a broad range of matters that are as a result unlikely to receive the attention they require for our effort to be as successful as we might wish.

In Chapter 8 we take what we have learnt about leadership context, vision, processes and focuses and use it to assist us to develop leadership impact for a school.

CHAPTER 8
Leadership impact

Leadership impact — **improving the performance and impact of the system.**

Measuring and improving leadership performance and impact at a school, in the context of improving school and student outcomes.

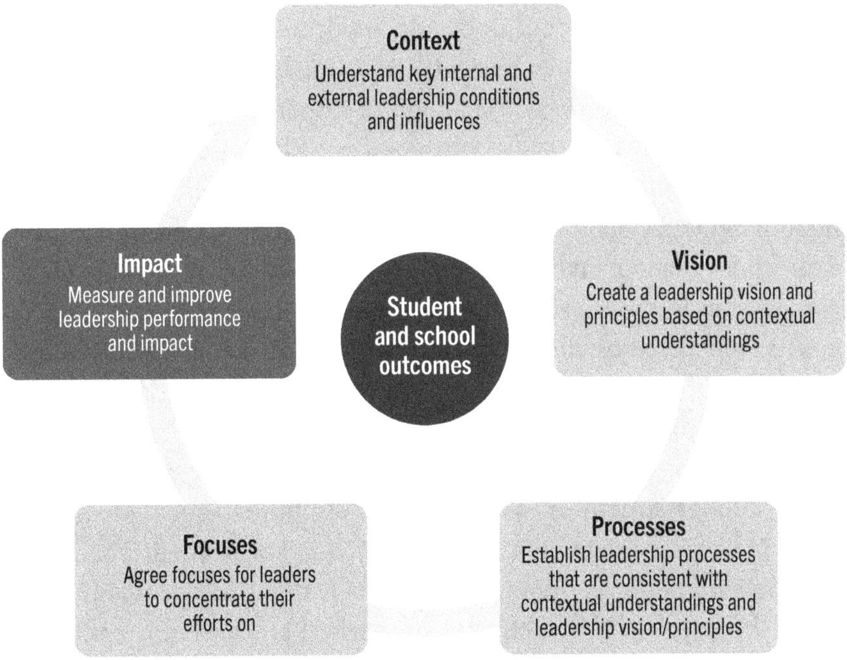

Context
Understand key internal and external leadership conditions and influences

Vision
Create a leadership vision and principles based on contextual understandings

Processes
Establish leadership processes that are consistent with contextual understandings and leadership vision/principles

Focuses
Agree focuses for leaders to concentrate their efforts on

Impact
Measure and improve leadership performance and impact

Student and school outcomes

Figure 8.1 Leadership impact

'Leadership impact' provides an opportunity to understand, manage and improve the effects of leadership within, across and beyond a school, with a central focus on improved school and student outcomes.

Leadership impact effort examines leadership inputs, outputs and outcomes to understand the impact of the school's leadership activity within, across and beyond the school. It provides a framework for setting, resourcing, developing, measuring and improving impact, to improve or transform the performance of leadership effort at the school and improve school and student outcomes.

It is important to note here that throughout this book I have referred to 'school and student outcomes'. While student outcomes should be a central focus, it might be that our approach to school improvement may not see positive outcomes for months or years as things are being implemented. Focusing on a variety of school outcomes can help us understand shorter term results, which can tell us if we are heading in the right direction to improve student outcomes. It is important to recognise that if students are achieving good outcomes, but teachers and the system are not, for example, the model might not be sustainable.

Natural ecosystems are constantly adjusting how they operate. Plants and animals in the ecosystem change in response to climate, weather and natural events, such as earthquakes. They are influenced by human activity and in response to their interaction with other species. In an integrated system like this, changes in the form and functioning of one species can often have a significant impact on one or more of the other species in the ecosystem (or other related ecosystems) and on the operation of the ecosystem more broadly. These changes can happen quickly (e.g. because of fire or disease), or over long periods of time (because of erosion or climate change).

On any project, strategy or initiative we are working on, we can set up all sorts of structures and processes, establish plans and develop vision and mission statements, but if we do not know whether the work is making a difference, then we are not really doing justice to our effort and to the purpose of that effort. How can we know what is and is not working? How can we adjust our approaches, our focuses, our strategies and the resourcing we are committing? How can we understand what we need to do to improve our effort, performance and impact?

Increasingly, over my 40 years in the education sector, understanding school performance and outcomes has become more prevalent, comprehensive and nuanced. As noted in the previous chapter, in the mid-1990s when I was an assistant principal, the education system here in Victoria introduced a new school strategic planning process, which had as its foundation the use of data and evidence through which to improve school performance. Our understanding and use of data and evidence was basic, but we certainly had a keen interest in learning how we were performing and using the information we gathered to direct our school's improvement energies. As discussed in Chapter 7, our planning usually led to too many focuses and priorities, but I believe that this time in our school system's development was critical for establishing an interest in data and evidence for improvement.

In my time at the Bastow Institute, we endeavoured to improve evaluating our performance as a professional learning organisation and understand our impact. While we collected information about how many people undertook our courses and attended our seminars, and we gathered participant views about their satisfaction with the learning they undertook, we also attempted to design an evaluation that measured the impact of a participant's learning on school and student outcomes. This was no easy task! As those more versed in evaluation science will tell you, proving a relationship between the work of a leader and an improvement in student learning is hard because of the number of other variables that exist between what the leader does and how the student performs. I will not go into detail about the methodology that was designed, other than to say that we used a proxy measure for understanding impact. We asked several of the participants' colleagues to report on the participants' leadership improvement because of undertaking learning at the Bastow Institute, and to indicate whether they believed that the learning had an impact on student outcomes at the school. Why did we want to collect evidence around the impact of the learning? We wanted to understand whether the investment was making a difference. We wanted to know which of our courses were improving a participant's leadership capacity so we could adjust and improve our performance in other courses. We wanted to be accountable for the spending of public monies, but most of all we wanted to improve student outcomes in schools and if we were not doing that then we needed to change what we were doing. Suffice to say that the evaluation demonstrated that we were having good impact overall, and it helped us identify where we could improve.

The question that arises here is, Do you know much about the impact of your leadership as an individual or as a team or as a group of leaders at your school? Are you making attempts to evaluate your leadership performance and its impact? Are the methods you are using providing accurate data and improving leadership practice? School leaders should know whether they are making a difference, how much difference they are making and whether their leadership effort is improving school and student outcomes. How is it possible to know these things, and how accurate is the methodology, data and evidence that is being used for understanding that impact? It is important to consider the way in which we understand leadership impact. We need to use relevant, accurate and up-to-date data. At its simplest, it is about understanding how well your leadership approach is working and what needs to change to improve it further.

Knowing the impact we are having is important, but we also need to understand what exactly is having an impact and what is not. We need to know whether that impact is sufficient, given the resources we are committing. We need to know if it is achieving the vision we have established and the specific performance indicators we have set for our leadership approach. We need to understand what needs to change and how best to make that change in order to improve leadership performance and impact.

The purpose of this chapter is not to provide a detailed exploration of evaluation methodology and techniques, but to provide a range of ideas for measuring your leadership performance and impact, for understanding whether your leadership effort is meeting your stated intentions, and for considering how to use the data and evidence you gather to improve leadership performance as an individual, a team, and/or a collective. This chapter examines the following 3 key ideas:

1. Measure performance and impact.
2. Use quality data and evidence.
3. Finalise the development of your leadership ecosystem.

1. Measure performance and impact

The 2 critical things to consider in looking at the performance of your leadership are: 'What' do you want to know and 'how' can you find it out?

There is a broad range of evaluation types depending upon the literature you are looking at. For example, the US Centers for Disease Control and Prevention (CDC)[1] considers the main forms to be:

- formative
- process/implementation
- outcome/effectiveness
- impact
- economic evaluation.

The New South Wales Government[2] education website lists 3 types: process, outcome and economic evaluation. While the list of types varies widely depending on the advice you are reading, the evaluation types described here cover most of those mentioned.

An 'evaluation approach' that encompasses formative, process, outcome and impact evaluation is likely to prove most useful. It should provide information about the fidelity of your leadership ecosystem implementation (formative/process evaluation), progress against the identified focuses (outcome evaluation), and effectiveness of the approach in improving school and student outcomes (impact evaluation). Where a school has not previously had a formal whole-school leadership approach, it might be useful to use a developmental[3] approach to evaluation, where implementation check points are built into the approach to allow for the collection of regular pulse-check data and evidence that can be used to pivot, change or adapt the approach if

---

1 CDC (Centers for Disease Control and Prevention) (2020) *Practical use of program evaluation among sexually transmitted disease (STD) programs*, Department of Health & Human Services, USA, accessed 12 February 2022. https://www.cdc.gov/std/program/pupestd.htm
2 NSW Government – Education (2022) *Types of evaluations*, accessed 21 February 2022. https://education.nsw.gov.au/teaching-and-learning/professional-learning/pl-resources/evaluation-resource-hub/evaluation-design-and-planning/types-of-evaluations
3 Better Evaluation (n.d.) *Developmental evaluation*, accessed 28 June 2022. https://www.betterevaluation.org/en/plan/approach/developmental_evaluation

something is not working. This approach is normally used for projects that are just beginning, or a model has not been proven to work in a particular context yet. It is similar to formative/process evaluation but has more of a focus on adapting a program as it is being implemented; it is traditionally used for large, complex social issues; but as we know, leadership can be complex.

A useful way to start might be to use a 'program logic approach'.[4] The WK Kellogg Foundation suggests that a 'logic model is a systematic and visual way to present and share your understanding of the relationships among the resources you have to operate your program, the activities you plan, and the changes or results you hope to achieve'.[5] Their Logic model development guide[6] provides a basic logic model (see Figure 8.2).

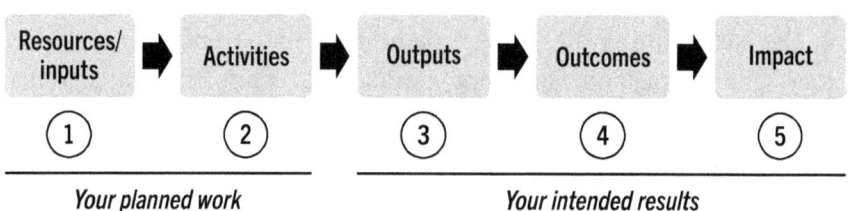

Figure 8.2 The basic logic model[7]

Using a logic model allows you to consider what you are putting into your leadership approach, how it operates and the impacts of your efforts. There is significant information available online and in various publications to assist you with using a logic model, so source an approach that will suit you and your school.

You may decide that a logic model does not suit your context or purposes and choose to find alternative models; as stated already in

---

4   See for example: Fritz J (2020) *How to talk about nonprofit impact from inputs to outcomes: inputs, outputs, outcomes, impact – how are they different?*, The Balance Small Business, accessed 23 February 2022. https://www.thebalancesmb.com/inputs-outputs-outcomes-impact-what-s-the-difference-2502227
5   WK Kellogg Foundation (2004:1) *Logic model development guide*, accessed 21 February 2022. https://www.betterevaluation.org/sites/default/files/LogicModelGuidepdf1.pdf
6   WK Kellogg Foundation (2004)
7   WK Kellogg Foundation (2004). Image reproduced with permission.

this chapter, there is extensive literature and advice on evaluation approaches that you could adapt to suit you and your school. Many of these approaches have common steps and use similar strategies; such as a balanced scorecard approach.[8] The important thing is that you establish a methodology to evaluate your leadership approach, that you find ways to understand how your leadership ecosystem is performing and the impact it is having and have sufficient information to improve you and/or your school's leadership effectiveness.

There are several practical considerations that are worth exploring as you develop your leadership ecosystem evaluation approach:

- The data and evidence you need will vary based on your leadership context, vision, principles, processes and focuses.
- Don't overdo it: develop an evaluation design that is manageable, even if you start small and grow the evaluation approach over time. You do not want to create something that is too big and unmanageable and almost impossible to implement.
- It is worth noting that measuring long-term impact is complex and expensive. Unless you have been well funded to do an impact evaluation and have access evaluation experts, it is advisable to start small and look for short- and medium-term outcomes that can inform leadership improvement.
- Don't underdo it: it is worth investing time and effort in understanding if, how and why your leadership approach is or is not working as well as expected. You owe it to yourself, your colleagues, the school community and your students to ensure your leadership is as good as it can be.
- Be transparent: ensure that the school community understands why you are collecting the information and share de-identified data and results openly.
- Use information or data that you may already be collecting, for example, parent, staff and student surveys, and student performance data. This could be used as it exists or adjusted

---

8   Balanced Scorecard Institute (2022). *How to create a balanced scorecard: nine steps to success*, accessed 2 February 2022. https://balancedscorecard.org/about/nine-steps/

to suit, for example by adding a question in the staff, parent or student survey specifically about whether there is consistent application of the leadership principles across the school.
- Add new data collection tools where required: for example, establishing focus groups to gather information about the implementation and performance of the leadership ecosystem or developing a parent survey where you do not currently have one.
- Establish a variety of good quality data sources, including a variety of quantitative and qualitative information. ACER, in describing how to use the Principal Performance Improvement Tool, argues that 'Principals can develop a deeper understanding of the effectiveness of their leadership by gathering feedback from multiple sources. These sources may include self-reflections, conversations with colleagues, input from mentors and responses to staff/parent/student surveys. The "triangulation" of input in this way increases the accuracy of conclusions based on the tool and minimises the impact of extraneous influences and possible biases.'[9] This approach should hold true for evaluating the performance and impact of your leadership approach.

2. Use quality data and evidence

Understanding how your leadership ecosystem is operating and the impact it is having provides a strong foundation for continuous improvement of the leadership system you have established. It should provide you with information about what needs to be adjusted to increase its operational efficiency and effectiveness and ensure that you are accountable to your school community and other important stakeholders for the efficacy of your leadership approach.

In Chapter 4 we briefly considered the importance of quality use of data and evidence and noted that the Q Project[10] suggests that it is not just a matter of having the right data and evidence, it is important that there is quality use of that evidence. 'Quality use of research evidence

---

9   ACER (2018a:3)
10 Monash University (2020a)

in education [is defined] as the thoughtful engagement with and implementation of appropriate research evidence, supported by a blend of individual and organisational enabling components within a complex system.'[11] The Q Project website[12] provides a range of information and resources that, while focused on the use of research evidence, might also provide some insights into the use of the data and evidence you gather regarding the performance and impact of your leadership ecosystem.

> Several years ago, I had the opportunity to work with a team of Bastow Institute colleagues to participate in a Data Wise Leadership Institute 5-day course that builds a team's capacity '... in using collaborative data inquiry to drive continuous improvement ...'[13] The focus of the program is usually for school teams to develop collaborative approaches for using data to improve student outcomes. Given that the Bastow Institute was not a school team per se, the focus for us was on improving our performance and impact through improved use of data and evidence. Involvement in the course introduced us to the Data Wise Improvement Process model, including a range of strategies, tools, practices and dispositions to create a more strategic and collaborative approach to organisational improvement. At the heart of the model is the Data Wise Improvement Process,[14] which focuses on collaborative teams. The process includes 3 key steps: prepare, inquire and act, and the resources provided are practical and well thought out. It is worth looking through the materials and professional learning available to see whether the approach and model
>
> Continued ▶

---

11 Monash University (2020b:1)
12 https://www.monash.edu/education/research/projects/qproject
13 Data Wise (n.d.) *Welcome to Data Wise*, Harvard Graduate School of Education, Harvard University, https://datawise.gse.harvard.edu/
14 Boudett KP, City EA and Murnane RJ (eds) (2013:5) *Data Wise: a step-by-step guide to using assessment results to improve teaching and learning*, revised and expanded edn, Harvard Education Press, Cambridge, MA; DET (Department of Education and Training) (2016) Victorian early years learning and development framework, Victoria Curriculum and Assessment Authority, accessed 29 July 2022. https://www.education.vic.gov.au > learning frameworks birth to 8 years; MindTools (n.d.) PDCA (Plan Do Check Act), accessed 12 May 2021. https://www.mindtools.com/pages/article/newPPM_89.htm

> might suit you and your school. I must say that one of the favourite protocols used by Data Wise is the use of the Ladder of Inference; I have found this to be a useful tool when working with data with others.

One of the challenges in using data and evidence well is choosing, creating and developing appropriate actions to address the findings in your data analysis, or alternatively, identifying and enacting change that will make the biggest difference. As Hattie suggests, 'Instead of asking "What works?" we should be asking "What works best?" as the answers to these questions are quite different ... the answer to the first question is "Almost everything" whereas the answer to the second is more circumscribed – and some things work better and some worse relative to the many possible alternatives.'[15]

The earlier chapters in this book have included a range of sources of evidence-based information about the efficacy of various leadership approaches, and leadership knowledge, skills and dispositions that are worth considering when identifying ways to improve your leadership ecosystem based on the data and evidence you have collected. For example, you might consider some of the online information on 'visible learning' by John Hattie[16], and a number of the collective school leadership references from Chapter 1, including West and colleagues,[17] Canwell and colleagues[18] and Leithwood and colleagues.[19] This is clearly not an exhaustive list, but it does provide a starting point for identifying leadership strategies that may meet the needs or changes identified in your analysis of your leadership data. There are also several sources of information about the efficacy of efforts for improving student outcomes, such as the Education Endowment Foundation fund,[20]

---

15 Hattie J (2008:18) *Visible learning: a synthesis of over 800 meta-analyses relating to achievement*, Routledge
16 Corwin (n.d.) *Accelerate student learning by focusing on what works best*, accessed 28 July 2022. https://au.corwin.com/en-gb/oce/visible-learning-0
17 West et al. (2015)
18 Canwell et al. (2018)
19 Leithwood et al. (2019)
20 Education Endowment Foundation (n.d.) *Education evidence*, accessed 27 July 2022. https://educationendowmentfoundation.org.uk/education-evidence

Evidence for Learning[21] and the What Works Clearinghouse.[22] These sorts of websites tend to focus on student learning strategies rather than leadership strategies and approaches, but you may well find some information in these websites and in others that relate to evidence about leadership practice and focuses.

In terms of using your leadership data and evidence to improve your ecosystem operation and leadership impact, several of the matters listed earlier in this chapter are worth reflecting on again, together with a few further considerations, such as:

- *Don't overdo it*: do not try to instigate too many changes at once; focus on the most important changes first and add others as resource, time and capacity for change allow. Play the long game, to avoid burning everyone out at the start.
- *Don't underdo it*: it is worth maintaining some urgency in terms of implementing improvement, but as in all things, balance is important.
- *Consult widely on what should change and how*: the whole point of a leadership ecosystem is to ensure collaborative and integrated action.
- *Be transparent*: ensure that the school community understands the changes that are being proposed and made, including what will change and how it will change.
- *Align with your context*: ensure that changes to your leadership ecosystem suit your individual, team, school and/or network context.
- *Be clear about the changes you are making*: if the improvements you are making are too complex, they may be hard to implement and could cause confusion for other leaders and school community members.

---

21 Evidence for Learning (n.d.) *Using the toolkits*, accessed 27 July 2022. https://evidenceforlearning.org.au/the-toolkits/about/
22 What Works Clearinghouse (n.d.) *What Works Clearinghouse*, accessed 26 September 2022. https://ies.ed.gov/ncee/wwc/

- *Don't change things if you don't need to*: there is no point in fixing something that is not broken; do not create change for change's sake.

Establish mechanisms to lead ecosystem adjustments and changes, and to ensure that they have the authority to endorse changes as required for the leadership vision, principles, processes, focuses and impact evaluation and to influence leadership context.

'Don't change things if you do not need to' is critical. Unless there is a mechanism for ongoing monitoring of the leadership information and data and for leading changes to the system, then the ecosystem will remain static and cease to improve. One possibility is to establish a team of leaders (formal and informal) from across the school that have responsibility for the monitoring and management of the leadership ecosystem. This could be an existing group or a newly formed group. In establishing such a group, it is worth considering the development of a mandate for the group; specifying its membership, role, operation and authorising environment.

Activity 15 provides guidance for establishing an evaluation approach to suit your particular context and using the evaluation to improve your leadership performance and impact.

> ### Activity 15: Establishing an approach to measure and improve your leadership performance and impact
>
> **Purpose:** To assist you to understand and improve the performance and impact of your leadership approach.
>
> **ACTIVITY**
>
> **Step 1:** Establish mechanisms to develop, lead and manage the evaluation approach and changes to the ecosystem.
>
> **Step 2:** Consider the purpose of measuring the impact of your leadership approach. What are the main reasons you want to measure leadership impact? And what are the main things you want to do with this information? Examples include:
>
> - to inform decision-making related to learning and improvement
> - to serve accountability needs of the school
> - to generate knowledge and document lessons learnt for others.

Step 3: Consider what the scope of your impact measurement is. What resources do you have to put towards data collection activities? Which stakeholders will be included: students, teachers, parents? Who is the audience of the impact data? How often do you want to reflect on the data? Over what period are you expecting to see change?

Step 4: Consider what you want to measure. This should include the leadership vision, principles, processes and focuses you have developed, and identified metrics or targets in your strategic plan. Consideration could also be given to measuring improvement in school and student outcomes; however, demonstrating a direct relationship between leadership activity and these outcomes might prove difficult. Careful investigation of evaluation literature and selecting a suitable approach might assist.

Step 5: Choose and document an approach that suits you and your school, and which is likely to provide the information you need accurately and as easily as possible. The approach is likely to include:

- clear objectives and steps for the approach
- identification of what are you attempting to measure
- identification of inputs and potential outcomes
- identification of new and existing data sources
- a schedule for collecting data
- an approach for recording and analysing your data
- timely and accurate analysis of the data.

Step 6: Undertake the evaluation and monitoring.

Step 7: Share the results of your evaluation with the school community and other key stakeholders.

Step 8: Use the results to inform changes to your leadership approach:

> **Step 8.1:** List the places where changes are indicated in your data and evidence.
>
> **Step 8.2:** Prioritise based on:
>
> - what is critical
> - what the research says
> - what is likely to work best in your context.
>
> **Step 8.3:** Use the results to inform changes to your leadership approach.

3. Finalise development of your leadership ecosystem

In Activity 16, take the information you developed as you worked through this chapter and add it to the activities from Chapters 4 to 7 to finalise development of a leadership ecosystem for yourself and/or your school. This includes documentation regarding your evaluation approach in Activity 15. As noted in Chapter 4, the activities provided here are an example of work you could undertake; there are many other exercises and processes that you could also work through to identify and monitor your leadership impact and improve leadership performance.

> **Activity 16: Building your leadership ecosystem – impact**
>
> **Purpose:** To further develop your leadership ecosystem overview by adding your leadership impact and improvement information to the leadership approach development work undertaken in preceding chapters of this book.
>
> **ACTIVITY**
>
> Add your leadership impact and improvement information to the overview document you started in Activity 5.

In Chapters 1 and 2, we identified leadership impact as one of the 5 ecosystem elements that can be used to assist us to develop a more systematic approach to leadership in a school, as summarised here.

> *Leadership impact*: measuring and improving leadership performance and impact at a school, in the context of improving school and student outcomes.
> - 'Leadership impact' provides an opportunity to understand, manage and improve the operation and impact of leadership within, across and beyond a school, with a central focus on improved student outcomes.
> - Understanding whether your leadership approach is operating effectively, what impact it is having on leadership efficacy across the school and understanding the impact it is (or is not) having on

improving school and student outcomes can assist in working out how to improve the school's leadership approach.
- Leadership impact provides a framework for setting, resourcing, developing, measuring and improving leadership performance and impact.

In Chapter 9 we explore how a school can integrate the various elements of the approach to develop a fit-for-purpose, context-aligned leadership ecosystem that is directly focused on improving school and student outcomes.

CHAPTER 9
An integrated leadership ecosystem

An 'integrated leadership ecosystem' speaks to the development of a localised school leadership system that is firmly based on the school's unique circumstances and context; an integrated, coherent and comprehensive system that brings together the collaborative and individual effort of all the school's leaders (staff, students and parents) and all leadership practice (formal and informal) at all levels of the school; a self-improving system that measures leadership performance and impact and adjusts for improvement; a system that is explicitly focused on improving school and student outcomes.

One of the things that I enjoyed as I progressed through school leadership roles was the chance to create new things, to restructure operations and processes, and to lead implementation of new or revised initiatives. I enjoyed the challenge of understanding what was needed and finding ways to meet that need; for me it was a creative endeavour that involved a lot of problem-solving and working with others to find and develop solutions. However, the joy of creating the new, and renovating the existing, can be problematic, as once the work of implementation is over and things become 'business as usual', I know that I must stay on task and not go looking for the next thing that I can develop and create. As noted earlier in this book, too often in education there is a tendency to move on to the next great idea before we have successfully implemented the last one; sometimes you need to 'go slow to go fast'.

The method for developing a school-wide leadership approach outlined in this book involves creating an integrated, coherent and comprehensive ecosystem; an interconnected system that is self-improving and focused on improving school and student outcomes. As mentioned in Chapter 1 'Leadership approaches' (p. 10), this is much more than undertaking ad hoc individual leadership exercises or engaging in team-building processes. It is about being systematic in how we agree to lead, how we 'actually' lead and how we know whether our leadership is making a difference. It is a planning, implementation and improvement approach for leadership within, across and beyond a school.

If you have worked through the suggested activities in this book, you will now have an 'overview document' that is a consolidated set of information about your own ecosystem leadership approach. It will outline your leadership context, vision, principles, processes, focuses and how leadership performance and impact will be used to build your leadership ecosystem. Well done: what an achievement! As has been discussed throughout this book, however, the ecosystem will not work effectively if it is not a dynamic, living, self-improving process. The overview document provides an explicit statement that can be used to ensure that the whole school community understands and aligns their formal and informal leadership practice with the school's agreed approach. It provides you with a foundation on which to continue to enhance leadership within, across and beyond the school.

The challenge now is to sustain and build on this leadership system to ensure it continues to improve its operation and impact, but most importantly, that it drives continuous improvement in school and student outcomes. Take the opportunity as you read through this final chapter to look at the results of the activities you have undertaken or things you have learnt. Consider whether there are aspects of your leadership approach that you wish to adjust, and/or that you might be interested in updating and to which you might apply some of the ideas from this book.

If you have not completed the activities in this book, then there are few options open to you. You could:

1. go back and work your way through the activities as they stand
2. take the ideas in the book and develop your own approach for the creation of a leadership ecosystem
3. hasten slowly and rather than jump into a structured project approach just work through the leadership context activities in Chapter 4 and develop a leadership vision using Chapter 5, and then sit with that until you are ready to move to the next steps in the process.

Most schools have extensive experience leading the development of new systems, processes and initiatives, and there may well be preferred project management strategies and approaches that are used. If the approaches you use are successful in your context, then it would be sensible to make use of those in developing a leadership ecosystem; there is no point starting over unnecessarily. Having said that, I would encourage you to work through this chapter to establish whether there is any advice or suggestions that might enhance your current approach, or in fact improve or replace strategies that are part of your approach. In my experience, there is always something new to learn across so many aspects of our lives, or sometimes information that you happen upon that you knew about but had forgotten.

Successful project management can provide us with comprehensive, efficient and effective ways to realise our goals. If, for example, we do not consult with stakeholders in an intentional and effective manner, then we risk the change not being supported or accepted by stakeholders. If we fail to plan adequately, then we may miss important steps or fail to understand the resources required for successful implementation. If we neglect to consider change management strategies, those affected may not be on board with the change.

If we are serious about implementing something new at a school, then we need to be serious about the effort we put into planning and managing that implementation.

While there will be not be one perfect way that suits all schools, there are principles, strategies and techniques that may be useful for many schools. In this chapter we look at the following:

1. Approaches to project management.
2. Principles to guide the development of an ecosystem.

1. Approaches to project management

In Chapter 2 'Implementing an ecosystem approach to school leadership' (p. 42), we mentioned some common project management methodologies and process including Agile, Scrum, Kanban practices; waterfall and PRINCE2.

The 'Agile' project management approach,[1] as the name suggests, is an approach that involves short cycles or 'sprints' that respond to information as it becomes available, or in which aspects of a project are broken down into small parts. Agile project management is often used in software development projects, and increasingly, for projects where it is important to be able to adjust the way in which the project is implemented as it develops.

'Scrum' developed out of Agile approaches and is one of the methodologies used within an Agile approach. Atlassian's Agile Coach suggests, 'Often thought of as an Agile project management framework, Scrum describes a set of meetings, tools and roles that work in concert to help teams structure and manage their work.'[2]

'Kanban' was developed by the Toyota Corporation in the 1940s: 'It uses a system of visual cues that let the project team know what is expected of tasks within the project in relation to quantity and quality as well as when the tasks are expected to be accomplished.'[3] Like Scrum, it is associated with Agile approaches to project management.[4]

'Waterfall' is a more sequenced approach to project management than the Agile approach. Leeron Hoory and Cassie Bottorff describe the approach as 'a linear form of project management ideal for projects where the end result is clearly established from the beginning of the project. The expectations for the project and the deliverables of each stage are clear and are required in order to progress to the next phase.'[5] This approach is a more traditional way of managing a project, and in my experience, used more often in schools than the Agile methodology.

'PRINCE2' methodology was used widely during my time working in government. It is a detailed approach with many steps, processes and tools. It is probably best suited to larger, more complex projects,

---

1   Adobe (2022) *Agile project management*, accessed 16 March 2022. https://www.workfront.com/project-management/methodologies/agile
2   Atlassian (n.d.) What is Scrum? Atlassian Agile Coach, accessed 16 March 2022. https://www.atlassian.com/agile/scrum
3   nutcache (n.d.)
4   smartsheet (n.d.) *Kanban*, accessed 16 March 2022. https://www.smartsheet.com/content-center/best-practices/project-management/project-management-guide/kanban-methodology
5   Hoory L and Bottorff C (2022) *Agile vs. waterfall: which project management methodology is the best for you?*, Forbes Advisor, accessed 28 July 2022. https://www.forbes.com/advisor/business/agile-vs-waterfall-methodology/

but it can be 'scaled' to suit individual projects. PRINCE2 explains the purpose of the methodology, 'To describe what a project should do and when, PRINCE2 has a series of processes. These cover all the activities needed on a project, from starting up to closing down.'[6]

This overview of project management approaches gives you an idea of whether the approaches, or aspects thereof, might be useful in your school and leadership context. There are detailed resources online based on these and other approaches that I would encourage you investigate further.

2. Principles to guide the development of an ecosystem

In Chapter 2 'Implementing an ecosystem approach to school leadership' (p. 42), a set of principles for developing a leadership ecosystem were outlined (see below). These are based on my experience in project management in schools, education policy development and implementation at the Bastow Institute, and on my exploration of the literature concerning project management.

Principles for developing a leadership ecosystem

- Use of best evidence and data
- Effective stakeholder engagement
- Clear and consistent communication
- A planned, documented and strategic approach
- Comprehensive evaluative processes
- Agile and flexible design and implementation
- Ensure students are at the centre of the design and implementation

The principles outlined here are not an exhaustive list and may not apply to every context or individual or group need. They do, however, provide a starting point on which to base your approach to developing a leadership ecosystem. A fuller explanation of each of the principles is provided here.

---

6   PRINCE2 (n.d.) *PRINCE2 methodology*, Prince2.com, accessed 16 March 2022. https://www.prince2.com/aus/prince2-methodology

Use of best evidence and data

It is important that the data and information we are using to understand the leadership context in a school and on which we will be making decisions about the design and development of our approach to leadership is as accurate, up to date, comprehensive and relevant as possible. As is often said, 'dirty data in; bad decisions out'. RingLead[7] reports that the 7 most common types of dirty data include duplicate data, outdated data, insecure data, incomplete data, inaccurate or incorrect data, inconsistent data, and too much data. While the types of dirty data listed here are focused on business, they do provide pointers for considering the data and information used to create a learning ecosystem. Chapter 8 'Measure performance and impact' (p. 123) provides some important advice about data and information, particularly measuring performance and impact.

Effective stakeholder engagement

A critical foundation for collective school leadership is that the characteristics of that leadership are 'owned' by both leaders and followers. While it can be hard to get total agreement about something among a large group of people (and sometimes even a small group), ensuring that everyone has an opportunity to contribute ideas and feel heard is critically important in getting broad acceptance and engagement. As noted in Chapter 6, it is important that leadership processes are developed in consultation with those who have a vested interest in the process and its outcomes to ensure that the process is 'owned' by key stakeholders. Also noted in Chapter 6 'Modify and enhance leadership processes' (p. 102), the OECD publication 'An implementation framework for effective change in schools' provides some good advice and a series of helpful guiding questions for effective stakeholder engagement.

---

7 RingLead (2021) 'The 7 most common types of dirty data (and how to clean them)', RingLead blog, accessed 17 March 2022. https://pipeline.zoominfo.com/operations/dirty-data-bottom-line

Clear and consistent communication

Too often in my own leadership I have neglected to communicate well with stakeholders (internal and external): staff, students, clients, other services, colleagues, parents, my bosses; and because of it, the work was not as effective. Often, I was only concerned about getting the work done and was not fully communicating what was happening. I was not focused on keeping people up to date with how things were going. When we fail to communicate, we leave people behind, create resentment and make people feel excluded, and we can miss opportunities to get support for the change we are leading. As noted in Chapter 6, processes should be 'clearly documented and communicated' to ensure that people understand the process and know what it is designed to do, how it operates and how they can interact with it. Good communication should be clear, concise, regular and targeted to the appropriate audience.

A planned, documented and strategic approach

While it is possible to 'over plan', not having an agreed, documented approach to modifying or developing a new school initiative, project or change often ends up ad hoc and is ineffectively and inefficiently implemented. People become confused about what is changing, how it is changing and how they can contribute to the change. Strategically documenting the 'why' and 'how' is a collective approach to leadership ensuring that people are on board with the purpose and process. This allows them to contribute in approved ways and provides everyone with guidance as the leadership approach is implemented. The project management methodologies described in 'Approaches to project management' above, are examples that can assist here, and a project management tool like Trello[8] can assist with documenting, organising, tracking and communicating change.

Comprehensive evaluative processes

As discussed in Chapter 8 'Measure performance and impact' (p. 123), there are several considerations for creating an evaluation approach that suits your school context, needs and aspirations. Chapter 6 'Modify and

---

8   Trello (n.d.)

enhance leadership process' (p. 102) looks at monitoring the change and impact once the leadership ecosystem is in 'business-as-usual' operation. It is important to know how well the change is operating, whether it is meeting the targets that have been set, whether it is having the desired impact, and whether further changes are required. Chapter 7 'Manage leadership focus effort' (p. 114) provides advice that can be used to manage the leadership ecosystem more broadly.

Agile and flexible design and implementation

As noted in 'Approaches to project management' above, project management requires a design that allows the process to adjust as implementation progresses. While it is important to remain true to the original project and change process design (so that people have confidence in the process as it was originally proposed), it is equally important to adjust the process if required.

Ensure students are at the centre of the design and implementation

If you break it down, the role of schools is quite simple really; they exist to support students to learn. All matters concerning finance, infrastructure, staffing, policy and so forth are there to make it happen as best it can. If we are not asking ourselves how every aspect of the school can be organised to improve student outcomes, then we are not as focused as we should be on the central purpose of the school. Developing a leadership ecosystem and all the decisions about 'what' that leadership approach includes and 'how' it operates should be based on how leadership will improve student outcomes.

Throughout this book I have used the term 'school and student outcomes'. I have done that deliberately, because in my mind, they are connected, but they are different. Improving school outcomes includes things like maximising resource availability and choice, improving the quality of teaching, developing a relevant curriculum, providing safe, secure and fit-for-purpose infrastructure. These school outcomes are important, as they provide an underlying basis for efforts more directly focused on improving student outcomes.

An endnote

The advice contained in this book can only ever be a starting point. It is what you do with your colleagues that is the hard work, the challenge and the joy. Endeavouring to create a leadership system that is inclusive, comprehensive and has impact on students' lives now and into the future; a system that creates great leadership within, across and beyond a school; and one that improves the performance and outcomes of that school is something worth striving for.

As with any new model, I expect that 'ecosystem leadership' is just the start of a journey for many of you to create great collaborative leadership in your schools and hopefully to share that experience to help others in their collaborative endeavours. I would encourage you contact me using the 'contact us' form at **www.esleadership.com/contact/** with your experiences (good, bad and indifferent) so we can share our learning and help others to create powerful systems of leadership.

We are creating an ecosystem, which is underpinned by collaborative endeavour. We need to honour this central notion of collaboration as we work on improving our leadership. Ecosystems should be collaboratively developed and sustained.

I wish you well on your journey with others. We are better together than alone.

References

ACER (Australian Council for Educational Research) (2018a) *Using the principal performance improvement Tool*, accessed 18 January 2022. https://research.acer.edu.au/tll_misc/31/

ACER (Australian Council for Educational Research) (2018b) *Principal performance improvement tool*, accessed 16 February 2022. https://research.acer.edu.au/cgi/viewcontent.cgi?article=1032&context=tll_misc

Adobe (2022) *Agile project management*, accessed 16 March 2022. https://www.workfront.com/project-management/methodologies/agile

Alexander W, Anderson M, Anterasian C and Lee J (2017) *Context matters: the five elements of context that most impact senior leader success*, SpencerStuart, accessed 9 June 2021. https://www.spencerstuart.com/research-and-insight/context-matters

Al Khajeh EH (2018) 'Impact of leadership styles on organizational performance', *Journal of Human Resources Management Research*, vol. 2018, article ID 687849, doi:10.5171/2018.687849

Allen K and Kern P (15 June 2018) 'School vision and mission statements should not be dismissed as empty words', *The Conversation*, accessed 11 June 2021. https://theconversation.com/school-vision-and-mission-statements-should-not-be-dismissed-as-empty-words-97375

Amanchukwu RN, Nwachukwu OP and Stanley GJ (2015) 'A review of leadership theories, principles and styles and their relevance to educational management', *Management*, 5(1):6–14, accessed 18 June 2020. http://article.sapub.org/10.5923.j.mm.20150501.02.html - Sec4.5

Amazon (2021) *Leadership principles*, accessed 29 July 2021. https://www.amazon.jobs/en/principles

Angelle PS and DeHart CA (2016) 'Comparison and evaluation of four models of teacher leadership', *Research in Educational Administration & Leadership*, 1(1):85–119.

Atlassian (n.d.) *What is Scrum? Atlassian Agile Coach*, accessed 16 March 2022. https://www.atlassian.com/agile/scrum

Bain & Company (2018) *Management tools: mission and vision statements*, Bain and Company Insights, accessed 17 June 2021. https://www.bain.com/insights/management-tools-mission-and-vision-statements/

Balanced Scorecard Institute (2022). *How to create a balanced scorecard: nine steps to success*, accessed 2 February 2022. https://balancedscorecard.org/about/nine-steps/

Barth RS (2006) 'Improving relationships within the schoolhouse', *Educational Leadership. Improving Professional Practice*, 63(6):8–13, http://www.ascd.org/publications/educational-leadership/mar06/vol63/num06/Improving-Relationships-Within-the-Schoolhouse.aspx

Becker B (2022) 'Leadership styles', *HubSpot blog*, accessed 12 July 2022. https://blog.hubspot.com/marketing/leadership-styles

Better Evaluation (n.d.) *Developmental evaluation*, accessed 28 June 2022. https://www.betterevaluation.org/en/plan/approach/developmental_evaluation

Biology Dictionary (n.d.) *Niche*, accessed 22 September 2020. https://biologydictionary.net/niche/

Bolívar B, López Yáñez JF and Murillo J (2013) *School leadership. A review of current research perspectives*, accessed 10 February 2021. https://repositorio.uam.es liderazgo en las instituciones educativas: una revisión de líneas de investigación.

Boudett KP, City EA and Murnane RJ (eds) (2013) *Data Wise: a step-by-step guide to using assessment results to improve teaching and learning, revised and expanded edn*, Harvard Education Press, Cambridge, MA.

Braun A, Ball S, Maguire M and Hoskins K (2011) 'Taking context seriously: towards explaining policy enactments in the secondary school', *Discourse: Studies in the Cultural Politics of Education* 32(4):585–596.

Brezicha K, Bergmark U and Mitra DL (2015) 'One size does not fit all: differentiating leadership to support', *Educational Administration Quarterly*, 51(1):96–132, doi.org/10.1177/0013161X14521632

Bridges WM (n.d.) *What is transition*, accessed 13 September 2022. https://wmbridges.com/about/what-is-transition/

Britannica (n.d.) *Ecosystem*, accessed 27 July 2020. https://www.britannica.com/science/ecosystem

Cameron E and Green M (2020) *Making sense of change management: a complete guide to the models, tools and techniques of organisational change*, 5th edn, Kogan Page Limited.

Canwell A, Rolland L and Cotton T (2018) 'Collective leadership: leading for value across organizational boundaries', *Global Leadership Forecast 2018*, DDI, The Conference Board and EY, accessed 4 August 2022. https://www.conference-board.org/publications/publicationdetail.cfm?publicationid=7717

Carter D (2012) *Leadership principles*, Mr Carter's Office, accessed 5 August 2022. https://dwightcarter.edublogs.org/2012/12/31/leadership-principles/

CDC (Centers for Disease Control and Prevention) (2020) *Practical use of program evaluation among sexually transmitted disease (STD) programs*, Department of Health & Human Services, USA, accessed 12 February 2022. https://www.cdc.gov/std/program/pupestd.htm

Chapin III FS, Matson PA and Mooney HA (2002) *Principles of terrestrial ecosystem ecology*, accessed 4 August 2020. *doi*:10.1007/978-1-4419-9504-9

Cleland EE (2011) 'Biodiversity and ecosystem stability', *Nature Education Knowledge*, 3(10):14

Corwin (n.d.) *Accelerate student learning by focusing on what works best*, accessed 28 July 2022. https://au.corwin.com/en-gb/oce/visible-learning-0

Cosner S, Whalen S, Richard M and Hebert M (2021) *Exploring educational ecosystems through the lens of intermediary organisations: insights for policy and practice*, WISE, Qatar Foundation, accessed 23 February 2022. https://www.wise-qatar.org/exploring-educational-ecosystems-through-the-lens-of-intermediary-organizations/

Cummings S, Bridgman T and Brown KG (2015) 'Unfreezing change as three steps: rethinking Kurt Lewin's legacy for change management', *human relations*, 69(1):33–60, doi:10.1177/0018726715577707

Data Wise (n.d.) *Welcome to Data Wise*, Harvard Graduate School of Education, Harvard University, accessed 13 September 2022. https://datawise.gse.harvard.edu/

Dell Technologies (n.d.) *How we work and lead*, accessed 8 July 2021. https://jobs.dell.com/how-we-work-and-lead

DET (Department of Education and Training) (2016) *Victorian early years learning and development framework*, Victoria Curriculum and Assessment Authority, accessed 29 July 2022. https://www.education.vic.gov.au/childhood/professionals/learning/Pages/veyldf.aspx

D'Innocenzo L, Mathieu, JE and Kukenberger MR (2014) 'A meta-analysis of different forms of shared leadership – team performance relations', *Journal of Management*, 1–28, doi:10.1177/0149206314525205

disc profile (n.d.) *What is DiSC: deepen your understanding of yourself and others*, accessed 27 July 2022. https://www.discprofile.com/what-is-disc/

Education Endowment Foundation (n.d.) *Education evidence*, accessed 27 July 2022. https://educationendowmentfoundation.org.uk/education-evidence

Evidence for Learning (n.d.) *Using the toolkits*, accessed 27 July 2022. https://evidenceforlearning.org.au/the-toolkits/about/

Four Rooms of Change (n.d.) *This is The Four Rooms of Change – the real deal that helps you manage change*, accessed 27 July 2022. https://fourroomsofchange.com/

Fox T (7 February 2013) 'Developing leadership principles', *The Washington Post*, accessed 14 July 2021. https://www.washingtonpost.com/national/on-leadership/developing-leadership-principles/2013/02/07/3ddf61e2-7171-11e2-ac36-3d8d9dcaa2e2_story.html

Friedrich TL, Vessey WB, Schuelke MJ, Ruark GA and Mumford MD (2011) *Technical report 1288. A framework for understanding collective leadership: the selective utilization of leader and team expertise within networks*, US Army Research Institute for the Behavioural and Social Sciences, accessed 29 July 2022. https://arit.sirsi.net/uhtbin/cgisirsi/?ps=4rp3rkEb1a/0/X/60/495/X > technical report 1288.

Fritz J (2020) *How to talk about nonprofit impact from inputs to outcomes: inputs, outputs, outcomes, impact – how are they different?*, The Balance Small Business, accessed 23 February 2022. https://www.thebalancesmb.com/inputs-outputs-outcomes-impact-what-s-the-difference-2502227

Fullan M and Quinn J (2016) *Coherence: the right drivers in action for schools, districts and systems*, Ontario Principals Council and Corwin, CA.

Groysberg B, McLean A and Nohria N (May 2006) 'Are leaders portable?' *Harvard Business Review*.

Hallinger P (2018) 'Bringing context out of the shadows of leadership', *Educational Management Administration & Leadership*, 46(1):5–24, doi.org/10.1177/1741143216670652

Hattie J (2008) *Visible learning: a synthesis of over 800 meta-analyses relating to achievement*, Routledge.

Hattie J (2015) 'High impact leadership', *Educational Leadership*, 72(5):36–40, http://www.ascd.org/publications/educational_leadership/feb15/vol72/num05/High-Impact_Leadership.aspx

Hendricks-Jackson L and Hawkes B (2017) *Nursing professional development review and resource manual*, 4th edn, American Nurses Association.

Hmieleski, KM, Cole, MS and Baron RA (2012) 'Shared authentic leadership and new venture performance', *Journal of Management*, 38:1476–1499, doi:10.1177/0149206311415419

Hogan Assessments (n.d.) *Hogan development survey*, accessed 28 July 2022. https://www.hoganassessments.com/assessment/hogan-development-survey/

Hoory L and Bottorff C (2022) *Agile vs. waterfall: which project management methodology is the best for you?*, Forbes Advisor, accessed 28 July 2022. https://www.forbes.com/advisor/business/agile-vs-waterfall-methodology/

Indeed Career Guide (2020) *Understanding the contingency theory of leadership*, Indeed.com, accessed 20 November 2020. https://www.indeed.com/career-advice/career-development/contingency-theory-of-leadership

Indeed Career Guide (2021) *What are leadership vision statements?*, Indeed.com, accessed 22 June 2021. https://www.indeed.com/career-advice/career-development/leadership-vision-statements

Indeed Editorial Team (2022) *Contingency theory of leadership: definition and models*, Indeed.com, accessed 28 July 2022. https://www.indeed.com/career-advice/career-development/contingency-theory-of-leadership

in the pursuit of wisdom (20 May 2011) 'Quote by Chuck Close', *in the pursuit of wisdom blog*, accessed 15 July 2021.

Islam J and Hu H (2012) 'A review of literature on contingency theory in managerial accounting', *African Journal of Business Management*, 6(15):5159–5164.

Kachaner N, King K and Stewart S (2016) *Four best practices for strategic planning*, Boston Consulting Group, accessed 26 July 2022. https://www.bcg.com/en-au/publications/2016/growth-four-best-practices-strategic-planning

Kirkpatrick S (2016) *Build a better vision statement: extending research with practical advice*, Lexington Books.

Kotter Inc (n.d.) *8-step process for leading change*, Kotter, accessed 28 July 2022. https://www.kotterinc.com/8-steps-process-for-leading-change/

Kozlowski WJ and Ilgen DR (2006) 'Enhancing the effectiveness of work groups and teams', *Psychological Science in the Public Interest*, 7(3):77–124, doi:10.1111/j.1529-1006.2006.00030.x

Leithwood K, Harris A and Hopkins D (2019) 'Seven strong claims about successful school leadership revisited', *School Leadership & Management*, 40(1):5–22, doi:10.1080/13632434.2019.1596077

Leithwood K, Sun J and Schumacker R (2020) 'How school leadership influences student learning: a test of "the four paths model"', *Educational Administration Quarterly*, 56(4):570–599, doi:10.1177/0013161X19878772

Lidow D (13 February 2017) 'A better way to set strategic priorities', *Harvard Business Review*, accessed 10 February 2022. https://hbr.org/2017/02/a-better-way-to-set-strategic-priorities

Marr B (n.d.) *How many strategic goals should a company have?*, Bernard Marr & Co, accessed 8 February 2022. https://bernardmarr.com/how-many-strategic-goals-should-a-company-have/

MindTools (n.d.) *PDCA (Plan Do Check Act)*, accessed 12 May 2021. https://www.mindtools.com/pages/article/newPPM_89.htm

Mombourquette C (2017) 'The role of vision in effective school leadership', *International Studies in Educational Administration, Journal of the Commonwealth Council for Educational Administration & Management*, 45(1).

Monash University (2020a) *Q Project: Improving the use of research evidence in Australian schools*, Monash University Faculty of Education, Victoria, Australia, accessed 15 September 2020. https://www.monash.edu/education/research/projects/qproject

Monash University (2020b) *Q Project: Quality use of research evidence framework – Summary*, Monash University Faculty of Education, Victoria, Australia, accessed 29 July 2022. https://www.monash.edu/education/research/projects/qproject/publications/quality-use-of-research-evidence-framework-qure-report

Mulder P (2018) *Ladder of Inference*, ToolsHero, accessed 2 June 2021. https://www.toolshero.com/decision-making/ladder-of-inference/

Munby S (2017) *Principled leadership in challenging times*, Victorian Academy of Teaching and Leadership, accessed 28 July 2022. https://www.academy.vic.gov.au/learning-resources/principled-leadership-challenging-times

National Research Council (2015) *Enhancing the effectiveness of team science*, The National Academies Press, Washington, DC.

NSW Government – Education (2022) Types of evaluations, accessed 21 February 2022. https://education.nsw.gov.au/teaching-and-learning/professional-learning/pl-resources/evaluation-resource-hub/evaluation-design-and-planning/types-of-evaluations

nutcache (n.d.) '8 top project management methods, approaches, techniques', *nutchache blog*, accessed 15 September 2020. https://www.nutcache.com/blog/8-top-project-management-approaches-methods-techniques/

O'Neill C and Brinkerhoff M (2018) 'Five elements of collective leadership', *Not-for-Profit Quarterly*, Boston, MA, accessed 24 June 2020. https://nonprofitquarterly.org/five-elements-collective-leadership/

OECD (Organisation for Economic Co-operation and Development) (2020a) 'An implementation framework for effective change in schools', *OECD Education Policy Perspectives*, no. 9, OECD Publishing, Paris, https://doi.org/10.1787/4fd4113f-en

OECD (Organisation for Economic Co-operation and Development) (2020b) *Chapter 1. What TALIS 2018 implies for policy, vol 2*, accessed 18 June 2020. https://doi.org/10.1787/19cf08df-en

Pont B (2020) 'A literature review of leadership policy reforms', *European Journal of Education*, 55(2):154–168, https://doi.org/10.1111/ejed.12398

PRINCE2 (n.d.) *PRINCE2 methodology*, Prince2.com, accessed 16 March 2022. https://www.prince2.com/aus/prince2-methodology

Prosci (n.d.) *The Prosci ADKAR model*, Prosci, accessed 28 July 2022. https://www.prosci.com/methodology/adkar

RingLead (2021) 'The 7 most common types of dirty data (and how to clean them)', *RingLead blog*, accessed 17 March 2022. https://pipeline.zoominfo.com/operations/dirty-data-bottom-line

Robinson VM, Lloyd, CA and Rowe KJ (2008) 'The impact of leadership on student outcomes: an analysis of the differential effects of leadership types', *Educational Administration Quarterly*, 44(5):635–674.

Rouse K (2020) *A school leader's guide to effective stakeholder engagement*, Bellwether Education Partners, accessed 9 June 2021. https://bellwethereducation.org/publication/school-leader's-guide-effective-stakeholder-engagement

Rowley C and Changeboard Team (2016) *Leadership and the importance of context*, Changeboard, accessed 4 August 2022. https://www.changeboard.com/article-details/15535/leadership-and-the-importance-of-context/

Sagoff M (2003) 'The plaza and the pendulum: two concepts of ecological science', *Biology & Philosophy*, 18:529–552, https://doi.org/10.1023/A:1025566804906

Schilling DR (2013) 'Knowledge doubling every 12 months, soon to be every 12 hours', *Industry Tap Into News*, accessed 25 November 2020. https://www.industrytap.com/knowledge-doubling-every-12-months-soon-to-be-every-12-hours/3950

Seashore LK, Leithwood K, Wahlstrom K and Anderson S (2010) *Learning from leadership learning: the links to improved student learning*, Wallace Foundation.

Sendjaya S (2017) *Why Australian businesses need to become servant leaders*, Impact, Monash Business School, accessed 23 June 2020. https://impact.monash.edu/leadership/why-australian-business-leaders-need-to-become-servant-leaders/

Shariff K and Davis-Peccoud J (2012) *Score your organization to improve decision effectiveness*, Bain & Company, accessed 5 July 2022. https://www.bain.com/insights/score-your-organization-ame-info/

Singh SB (2019) 'Book review: How school leaders contribute to student success: the four paths framework', *School Leadership & Management*, 39(5):561–564, doi:10.1080/13632434.2018.1523143

smartsheet (n.d.) *Kanban*, accessed 16 March 2022. https://www.smartsheet.com/content-center/best-practices/project-management/project-management-guide/kanban-methodology

Stollar S, Poth R, Curtis M and Cohen R (2006) 'Collaborative strategic planning as illustration of the principles of systems change', *School Psychology Review*, 35(2):181–197.

The Ethics Centre (2020) *What is ethics?*, accessed 28 July 2022. https://www.youtube.com/watch?v=u399XmkjeXo

The Myers-Briggs Company (n.d.) *All about the Myers-Briggs (MBTI) assessment*, accessed 28 July 2022. https://ap.themyersbriggs.com/themyersbriggs-all-about-the-mbti-assessment.aspx

Trello (n.d.) *Trello helps teams move work forward*, accessed 28 July 2022. https://trello.com/home

Vold T and DA Buffett (eds) (2008) *Ecological concepts, principles and applications to conservation*, Bio Diversity BC, accessed 29 July 2022. http://www.biodiversitybc.org > ecological concepts 2008.

Wageman R, Nunes D, Burruss J and Hackman R (2008) *Senior leadership teams: what it takes to make them great*, Harvard Business School Press, Boston, MA.

Weber M (2021) *The 5 most vital strategic planning priorities for renewed focus and growth in 2022*, CUInsight, accessed 27 July 2022. https://www.cuinsight.com/the-5-most-vital-strategic-planning-priorities-for-renewed-focus-growth-in-2022.html

West M, Armit K, Loewenthal L, Ecker R, West T and Lee A (2015) *Leadership and leadership development in healthcare: the evidence base*, Faculty of Medical Leadership and Management, London, UK, accessed 29 July 2022. www.kingsfund.org.uk > leadership development health care.

West M, Lyubovnikova J, Eckert R and Denis J-L (2014) 'Collective leadership for cultures of high quality health care', *Journal of Organizational Effectiveness: People and Performance*, 1(3):240–260.

What Works Clearinghouse (n.d.) https://ies.ed.gov/ncee/wwc/, accessed 13 September. https://ies.ed.gov/ncee/wwc/

WK Kellogg Foundation (2004) *Logic model development guide,* accessed 21 February 2022. https://www.betterevaluation.org/sites/default/files/LogicModelGuidepdf1.pdf

Yasir M, Imran R, Irshad MK, Mohamed NA and Khan MM (2016) 'Leadership styles in relation to employees' trust and organizational change capacity: evidence from non-profit organizations', *SAGE Open,* doi:10.1177/2158244016675396

ZenDesk (n.d.) 'Change management models', ZenDesk blog, accessed 28 July 2022. https://www.zendesk.com/blog/change-management-models/

www.ingramcontent.com/pod-product-compliance
Lightning Source LLC
Chambersburg PA
CBHW052047070526
44584CB00017B/2085